Crises and
Special Problems
in Psychoanalysis
and Psychotherapy

Crises and Special Problems in Psychoanalysis and Psychotherapy

by

Leopold Bellak, M.D.

with

Peri Faithorn, M.D.

and the assistance of
Peter C. Plishka, M.D.

JASON ARONSON INC.
Northvale, New Jersey
London

THE MASTER WORK SERIES

First softcover edition 1994

ISBN: 1-56821-351-4
Library of Congress Catalog Card Number: 94-72438

Manufactured in the United States of America. Jason Aronson Inc. offers books and cassettes. For information and catalog write to Jason Aronson Inc., 230 Livingston Street, Northvale, New Jersey 07647.

TO

PAUL R. ESSERMAN
W. ERNST FREUD
MARGA and PHILLIPP RIEGER
SAUL SCHEIDLINGER

For nearly a lifetime of
loyalty and friendship
in crises and good times

Acknowledgments

This volume had its origin in a seminar I taught in the Post-doctoral Program in Psychotherapy at New York University Graduate School. Mary Ellen Beveridge, a professional writer and editor, sat in on the seminar and tape recorded, transcribed, and edited the material.

Thereafter, Peter C. Plishka, M.D. went over the entire manuscript and helped bring more order and organization to the book. Helen Siegel, M.A. further helped revise the text.

Finally, Peri Faithorn, M.D., in collaboration with me, re-organized, revised, edited and added some thoughts of her own, making a basic contribution to this book.

I am also grateful to my friend and colleague, M. Donald Coleman, M.D., who encouraged me to persevere with this project, and made some valuable comments, which I address myself to in the Introduction.

Inevitably, this book draws on my own experience and in some parts on previously published material dealing with subject matters related to the ones in this volume in another context, and, at times, published together with friends and colleagues. Wherever and whenever possible, footnotes acknowledge the appropriate sources.

I am also indebted to the staff of the A. A. Brill Library of the New York Psychoanalytic Institute and to Silvia Davidson and other staff members of the Department of Psychiatry Library of the Albert Einstein College of Medicine.

Contents

Introduction

Psychoanalysis as practiced today addresses itself not only to psychoneuroses, but also, and in fact increasingly, to character disorders, borderline conditions, and psychoses. The greater incidence of these latter psychopathological phenomena may, however, be more apparent than real. As psychoanalytic theory, diagnostic methods and acumen continue to develop, we may simply be recognizing conditions which have existed all along but have hitherto gone relatively unnoticed or, at least, have not been well understood. It may also be that the evolution of our culture, with its greater mobility, faster pace, less traditional concepts of family ("alternate life-styles") and consequently more frequently interrupted or disrupted human relationships, contributes to producing more of these varied types of emotional disturbances. Matters of a political, social, and professional nature, for example, patients brought to us by third-party payers, or the flood of recent publications on "borderlines," also undoubtedly have their influence on psychoanalytic practice, both in terms of *whom* we see and *how* we view them: The latter may often lead to an overdiagnosis of the so-called borderline condition. Psychiatry, like every other field, has its fads.

Whether or not there are in fact more of these varied therapeutic problems or whether we are better able to perceive or less able to ignore them, we all treat patients who are not "classical" neurotics. Though crises and special problems can and do occur in strictly classical psychoanalyses of the psychoneuroses, they occur even more frequently in other conditions. Almost by definition, the assets of patients with more complicated therapeutic problems will be fewer and the liabilities greater, whatever axis or combination of axes of evaluation and diagnosis one devises. These individuals are likely to have more poorly functioning psychic mechanisms, as well as fewer resources of an interpersonal, social or adaptive kind, because of their poorer endowments at all levels.

Some therapeutic techniques, notably some forms of object relations therapy of borderline states, utilize the patient's disorganization as a basis for his reconstituting in the transference situation. They are, however, at best long, drawn-out therapies, dependent on vast financial resources and involving an entire therapeutic team.

Dealing more practically with the more disturbed patient, whatever the label, often involves the judicious temporary suspension of therapeutic neutrality. Therapeutic ministrations will need to be more active and real, often without the luxury of distance. Concrete corrective emotional experiences, identification and introjection through which some of the unlearning, learning, and relearning takes place, are often a necessary part of the therapeutic process in order to offset or counter the effects of problematic or damaging early life experiences. Such untoward events and interactions have distorted these patients' view of the "real" world and led to maladaptive ways of shaping their ongoing life experience. Until effective restructuring and relearning have taken place, the therapist at times must be willing to lend the patient "prosthetic" ego functions in order to minimize occasionally irreversible ravages of these maladaptive patterns. In due time, it will be necessary to reanalyze the meaning and effect of the active intervention on the transference relationship.

Theoretically, crises should not arise if we have rigorously exercised our knowledge and skills with an eye to their anticipation and prevention; however, there is nothing the best psychoanalyst can do to avoid some acute difficulties. He cannot control reality and its vicissitudes. We must, therefore, be prepared to deal expertly with such events when they do occur. People become ill, financial reverses occur, and all sorts of other extrinsic life stresses tax the psychic energies and may have a disruptive intercurrent effect on an analysis or analytic psychotherapy. We can neither protect nor insulate patients from extrinsic problems, but we can certainly anticipate them and be prepared to help patients deal with them appropriately.

There is a long list of critical life situations in analysis which occur as part of the analytic process itself. There is no effective therapy without possible risks! These intrinsic crises may erupt despite all our understanding, knowledge, capacity to predict, and skills at intervention, and may lead to serious regressions, including psychotic ones. It is our responsibility to do whatever is appropriate and necessary to avoid dangers resulting from the analytic or psychotherapeutic process. An extensive knowledge of the patient's life situation, a very clear conceptualization of his psychic structure and dynamics and their relationship to the current problems, and a clear formulation and careful *planning* of the *areas, methods,* and *sequences* of intervention are essential. These are predicated upon a thorough grounding in 1) a general theory of psychology (here a psychoanalytic one), 2) a general theory of psychopathology, and 3) a general theory of psychotherapy based on the preceding two. As the surgeon must have a clear picture of anatomy, physiology, and pathology in a condition tentatively diagnosed, and a definite frame of reference for the therapeutic technique to be employed, so the psychotherapist must be precise and systematic when performing his verbal operations. The psychotherapeutic process and relationship have principles, rights, and responsibilities which ought not be left to hoping it will "all come out in the wash." To the extent to which this volume addresses itself to planning the therapeutic process, it could be said to attempt to make this process more efficient. Curiously enough, great as the development of psychoanalysis has been in many respects, I would be hard put to find a single publication which concerns itself with an increase in efficiency—in terms of shortening the process. I am excluding here the early attempts Ferenczi (1920) made, and those of Alexander and French (1946) which, like my own later attempts, must be seen more as brief psychotherapy rather than psychoanalysis proper.

Somehow, the idea of modifying the psychoanalytic process by introducing "parameters" has been anathema, considered akin to treason. And yet, to the extent to which everybody agrees that the basic process of therapy is a form of learning by insight, working through and restructuring by introjection and identification, it must be theoretically possible to improve the learning technique by various and different measures in different people.

Of course, activity, giving up therapeutic neutrality, is not without drawbacks. A good therapist often has to make judicious choices of priorities, in all fields of healing. Every potent drug is given in the hope that the advantages outweigh possibly dangerous side-effects. I am grateful to my friend and colleague, M. Donald Coleman, M.D., for pointing out that some of my suggested stratagems could be misunderstood or misused, especially by the relatively inexperienced— namely, as inappropriate intrusions into the therapeutic process and the rights of our patients. Let me, therefore, make clear here, as well as in various parts of the book, that all other things being equal, *the most appropriate and useful attitude of the psychoanalytic therapist*—in psychoanalysis proper or in any form of psychoanalytic psychotherapy—*is to observe therapeutic neutrality*. Only when there are special indications, such as discussed in this volume, is departure from this neutrality indicated.

On the other hand, I am writing this volume, among other reasons, because I have seen at least as much damage from inappropriate *failure* to intervene actively because of a failure to conceptualize and because of a confusing of the nature of therapeutic neutrality, dogmatic rigidity or passivity with an observant attitude. *It is as important to abandon therapeutic neutrality under special circumstances as it is to observe it in all ordinary psychotherapeutic situations.*

I hope that this volume, drawing on my own clinical experience of over three decades, as well as on supervising and teaching in various settings, will help some others in dealing *appropriately* with crisis and special situations.

L.B.

REFERENCES

ALEXANDER, F. & FRENCH, T. *Psychoanalytic Therapy*. New York: Ronald Press, 1946.
Arden House Conference, Harriman, New York, May 1954. The Widening Scope of Indications for Psychoanalysis. *Journal of the American Psychoanalytic Association*, Oct. 1954. Vol. 2. pages 565-620. (Leo Stone, Edith Jacobson, Anna Freud)
FERENCZI, S. The further development of an active therapy in psychoanalysis (1920). In *Further Contributions to the Theory and Technique of Psychoanalysis* by Ferenczi, S. London: Hogarth Press, 1950.

Crises and
Special Problems
in Psychoanalysis
and Psychotherapy

I. Basic
Principles

One of my favorite stories involves a general whose car broke down on maneuvers. When none of the army mechanics were able to fix it, an old village smith was asked to help. He lifted the hood, examined the engine, and then gave the distributor cap a sharp blow with his fist. Immediately, the motor started up. The general asked, "What do I owe you?" The village smith replied, "A hundred bucks." "A hundred bucks for one bang?" asked the general. "No," replied the smith, "One buck for the bang, ninety-nine for knowing *where* to bang."

This story illustrates the purpose of Part I of this volume. Before initiating therapy, one should know a great deal about the patient. The better one's overall understanding of the basic principles of the patient's makeup, the relatively easier it is to avoid crises and promote healing.

1. The Therapeutic Relationship

All psychotherapy is a form of unlearning, learning, and relearning, by insight, conditioning, and identification/internalization. Optimal circumstances for this unlearning, learning, relearning, in the "therapeutic relationship," are defined by the somewhat less broad and more manageable subdivisions probably most commonly labeled (a) the transference/countertransference relationship, (b) the therapeutic alliance, and (c) the therapeutic contract. Initially and fundamentally, we are responsible for initiating and facilitating the therapeutic process—the first task and potential problem or crisis in any therapy.

THE TRANSFERENCE/COUNTERTRANSFERENCE RELATIONSHIP

In the broad meaning of the terms "transference relationship," the patient comes with certain apperceptive distortions derived from the past, which he ascribes to the as yet unknown therapist, as suggested, for example, in his dreaming of going to the dentist the night preceding his first session. Certainly, more personal transference/countertransference relations form as soon as the patient and therapist meet in the waiting room, however much neutrality may be striven for.

In the initial interview, the patient and therapist are talking as intelligent co-equal adults. Once treatment begins, there will be time for technical neutrality, providing an unstructured field in which the patient's feelings and conflicts can emerge. Initially, the therapist's understanding attitude is important in motivating the patient to enter treatment if he or she needs it. If the patient does not pick up at least a slightly positive attitude from the therapist, he may well be driven to a friendly, but possibly incompetent, therapist of other persuasions. It is also important initially to give the patient at least an intellectual understanding of his problem(s), thus decreasing his feelings of helplessness and establishing feelings of hope. Intense interest in the patient's history, actively pursued, *guided by heuristic hunches*, serves the patient as a form of narcissistic gratification that strengthens the positive transference (and also provides the therapist with his fundamental data—see Chapter 2 on Anamnesis and Assessment).

The therapist might create an overall atmosphere of *compassionate empathy*, maintained sincerely by a view of life borrowed, like so much of psychoanalysis, from Greek drama, in which we are all more or less hapless victims of circumstances to which we adapt in various ways, more or less successfully. This will inspire in the patient a willingness to work with the therapist within the realistic limitations of the therapeutic alliance and contract. Positive and negative transference elements also influence the patient's willingness—or hesitancy —to form a therapeutic alliance and have a continued impact on the therapeutic process. Recognition and interpretation of these transference elements are crucial in crises intervention, just as in any other dynamic therapy.

Positive and/or negative countertransference feelings also tend to emerge in crises even more so than at other times. Positive countertransference feelings may emerge more or less in the form of a rescue fantasy; negative countertransference feelings may take such forms as critical feelings and premature cognitive closure. But such countertransference feelings can actually be quite helpful in understanding the patient if the therapist is not too threatened by them and not too obsessive to be emotionally available and therapeutically active where appropriate. This is the case where initiating therapy or initiating focused work on a specific problem or crisis in an ongoing treatment.

THE THERAPEUTIC ALLIANCE

The therapeutic alliance may be explained to the patient thusly: "The rational and intelligent part of you needs to sit together with me, the therapist, and together we must examine and understand the irrational unconscious part of you which causes you problems."

To help the patient understand the significance of this part of the therapeutic process, it is important to explain some basic ideas: There is a continuity between childhood and adulthood, between waking (conscious experience) and sleeping (unconscious phenomena), and between normal and pathological behavior. An illustration or two from the patient's own experience can be most effective. Dreams are especially valuable for this purpose. An account of how the patient acquired his particular dynamics and structure via apperception, apperceptive distortions and role identifications is also vital for his understanding of himself and the therapeutic process. The experiential process is like the laying down of thousands of transparencies, one on top of the other, e.g., of mother feeding, of mother cleaning, of mother punishing, all fused with pictures of other significant people in the patient's life. It is crucial that the patient appreciate that his contemporary apperception is structured to a greater or lesser degree by the Gestalten acquired in the past.

The success of therapy generally depends to a large extent on the ability of a part of the patient to work in alliance with the therapist on these issues. In a crisis, however, it must be clear that it is mostly the therapist's job to lead the way toward an understanding of these issues and processes. It is analogous to driving a car: The therapist gives gas, puts on the brakes, and turns the wheel; the patient is the motor. A selective inattention or dilution by a little more general talking will difuse and prevent anxiety, while, on the other hand, silence and interpretation of defenses will permit a conflict to surface and thus raise anxiety. These are some of the main instruments the therapist can employ to control the therapeutic process. They are the tools he uses to do the work involved in his part of the therapeutic alliance.

Many people are not accustomed to the associative process involved in good analytic reporting. This "internal travelogue" quality is captured in an anecdote about a delinquent who, when asked if he knew what a psychiatrist was, replied, "Yeah, that's someone who makes you squeal on yourself!" Patients are expected to squeal on themselves, in a sense—to tell things they observe about themselves. Despite facile explanations and analogies, this is often difficult, especially for patients in crisis. A concrete account of their day, an "external travelogue," can sometimes be shifted to an internal one. A standard set of questions can help the patient report on his inner life and make a contribution to the therapeutic alliance. For example, what was he thinking while engaged in any number of semi-automatic tasks, such as driving, shaving, or making up? What was the last thought before he fell asleep, or what was the first thing he thought on awaking? Again, it is the responsibility of the therapist to facilitate the therapeutic process.

In treating a broad spectrum of patients and problems, aside from employing standard therapeutic operations, the therapist may want to modify the superego, the ego-ideal and introjects, and the ego functions, where such intervention is dictated by the pathology and the emergent problems. This is often best achieved by directly lending himself as the modifier, where he may tell stories about himself or offer opinions, contrary to the customary stance of neutrality in psychoanalysis or prolonged psychotherapy. Often, older, more experienced therapists will confide using this more flexible approach, while younger therapists cling rigidly to dogma and incur a high treatment-failure and dropout rate. Vivid stories with colorful imagery, delivered in an understated way, convey certain ideas most effectively. It is a valid part of technique to have a suitable style likely to facilitate optimal learning in the given diagnostic and functional category. For example, to make some narcissistic behavior ego-alien, the therapist might tell the story of the millionaire and the bum. The bum is telling the rich man the story of his life. As the tears roll down the millionaire's cheeks, he finally reaches for the bell to summon his butler. As the bum's hopes soar and the butler appears, the millionaire turns to him and says, "Throw the bum out—he's breaking my heart."

GOALS AND THE THERAPEUTIC CONTRACT

Perhaps the central issue in terms of initiating and facilitating the therapeutic process, and yet probably the one which is least clearly presented by most therapists, is the definition of treatment goals. The patient is there implicitly because he believes the therapist knows what needs to be done and has acquired the necessary qualifications to achieve these ends. It is the therapist's responsibility to do whatever is appropriate and necessary, while avoiding unnecessary danger.

Under certain circumstances, the therapist must make vital and active decisions in the patient's best interest which the patient himself, by virtue of his pathology, is unable to make. Such interventions, for example, might include changing an ego-syntonic obsessive character into a manifestly more conflicted person, on the way to the hoped for resolution. They might also involve a prohibition designed to circumvent harmful acting-out, or perhaps enlisting the support or aid of a third party with the patient's knowledge, although at times without his initial consent, in order to offset a potential catastrophe. Hospitalization is also a course used at times to insure the patient's safety, even against his will. These circumstances may be compared to that of the surgeon when, once the patient has chosen to place his trust in him, has signed on the dotted line and is on the operating table, the physician must do whatever he deems necessary to cure his condition and maintain his safety.

At the same time, the therapist must motivate the patient to give the therapy a chance to achieve optimal results. He must convey the idea that the "good patient" gives up secondary gains and passivity. Clearly, this is a situation in which behavior therapists would consider it appropriate to reward or positively reinforce the relinquishing of such gratifications. So, as in other respects in initiating therapy or dealing with specific problems or crises, the therapeutic contract should be clearly and specifically stated. The more realistically one defines the therapeutic goals, the less the likelihood of disappointment leading to future crises, or to termination of the therapy altogether. Analysis cannot change reality. Certain problems of a life situation or expectation may well represent a major obstacle. Likewise, certain pathological elements may not always be subject to change and complete resolution. However, one *can* reasonably expect a better adaptation, a decrease or loss of symptoms, and a better functioning in most areas of life.

How long will therapy last? What is the prognosis? These are reasonable questions which are, however, difficult to answer and are often evaded by therapists. In fact, it is often not possible to give exact answers. However, an attempt should be made to offer an informal opinion or estimate based on the initial impression of the patient's assets and liabilities and of the possible reversibility or irreversibility of problems. The therapist's job is to help the patient achieve a better adaptation than he had achieved before. When it becomes evident that a particular approach is *not* helping the patient achieve the therapeutic goals, some other approach should be suggested and facilitated, including outside consultation co-therapy (e.g., concurrent treatment with another therapist for purposes of diluting the transference), or sometimes even transferring to another therapist altogether.

In addition to definition of treatment goals, clarification of other aspects of the working contract is also essential. This is true with any patient, but especially with more limited patients whose tolerance for ambiguity and frustration is bound to be low. The clearer the contract, the less likely that problems will arise later on. Everything should be discussed and clear pictures drawn. The therapist should not feel it is beneath his dignity to explain certain basic facts about the profession. The facts of the economic life of the psychotherapist are not usually clear to the general public. Times and fees, responsibility for broken appointments, vacations and illnesses are matters about which the therapist must define his positions. These must be communicated to the patient at the outset. The contract should not be considered to provide a guaranteed income for the therapist. It is untenable to oblige a patient to suit his vacation to the analyst's if this timing will cause the patient serious financial, personal or practical problems, or to charge a seriously physically ill patient for missed sessions, provided the "acting-out" potential of these and other issues is understood. Uncertainty with regard to the working contract may provide too fertile a ground for patients whose limited adaptive capacities and maladaptive mechanisms form the seeds of problems and crises. The limits of the therapeutic relationship can be clear without being rigid.

SUMMARY

Within this explicit conceptual framework, embedded in the psychoanalytic theory of personality, the theory of psychopathology, and the theory of therapeutic technique, the therapist will gather and assess the data for traditional therapeutic work. In addition, he should also be able to *anticipate* (see Chapter 2) and *plan* skillful, rational and humane therapeutic interventions (see Chapter 4), providing for an irreducible minimum of problems and/or crises, and the sequelae thereof in the course of therapy. This is a crucial aspect of treatment, whatever the level of the patient's pathology. It is an aphorism in medicine that if you don't know what you are looking for, you won't see it, the diagnosis will be missed, the inappropriate treatment administered, and the patient will suffer—and inevitably the doctor will suffer as well. Rigorous application of principles, professional responsibility, and therapeutic readiness will do much to prevent unpleasant surprises.

2. Anamnesis and Assessment

Given an adequate pool of relevant and meaningful data readily gathered by a well trained therapist with a good clinical eye, a patient's critical problems can be clearly conceptualized within a useful framework of clinical experience and theoretical knowledge. This is not placing a greater demand on the psychotherapist than one would make on any medical practitioner. The psychotherapist must approach the patient and his problem from a general outline or perspective, heuristically, while remaining flexible so that he may select a therapeutic strategy which provides for the best possible fit to the circumstances.

Like the microbiologist who peers through his microscope equipped with a body of knowledge and having certain expectations which help him see what is there, the psychotherapist is able to make a formulation of the general dynamics and structure of the patient's condition based on a detailed history and direct observations obtained in the first session. It is then his job to design a treatment plan which addresses itself specifically to the identified problem areas. He must outline specific methods and sequences of interventions which he feels will be most effective within a broad outline of a therapeusis derived from his own general propositions of structure, function, and psychopathology.

ANAMNESIS

The history should be as lively and concrete as possible, with especially careful attention paid to obtaining a clear understanding of the *chief complaint* (what, from a subjective standpoint, does the patient feel is wrong?), the *precipitating events* (what brings the patient to therapy today, rather than yesterday or last month; what is the difficulty or crisis *now*?) and the *current life situation* (what is the nature of the transference/countertransference relationship and what were the events in the last session(s), and the intercurrent events between sessions?). The chief complaint, precipitating events and current life situation should all be viewed against the backdrop of a vivid overall life history. One's grasp of this history should be such that it permits an almost dramatic visualization of the *settings, significant people, events,* and *interactions* at various times of life, and the degrees of impact of these circumstances, people, and events. One must be able to imagine in detail where the patient grew up, what the physical conditions were, who was around or not around, what was happening when this person was three years old, five years old, eight, twelve.

For example, a history of past experience or experiences with violence is crucial. A particular experience that brings the patient to us has to be seen in relation to earlier insults to his or her integrity, at the hands of an older sibling, a parent or others. The specific features of the assault have to be seen and understood in relationship to specific resultant or preexisting personality problems, such as fears of castration, poorly defined boundaries, or (psychic) helplessness and vulnerability. In any and all instances, treatment consists of helping the patient perceive the contemporary problem in terms of the past and the present. In adapting to this current problem, the patient acquires new strength, working through an old problem and finding a better form of dealing with it than existed premorbidly.

ASSESSMENT

As this historical data base is being gathered and distilled, the therapist is being guided by informed and lawful expectations. For example, in a depression, one would expect that one or more of a number of possible factors may play a dominant or significant role: 1) problems of self-esteem; 2) aggression in the presence of a severe superego manifesting itself primarily as intra-aggression; 3) a feeling of loss of a love object or of part of oneself; 4) a feeling of disappointment or of having been deceived (a variation of loss); 5) stimulus-hunger (deprived orality); 6) grossly deficient personality structures or functions, such as chronically depressed or narcissistic types; 7) a family history of depression; and 8) a medical history—a variety of physical disorders could play a role in a depression (as well as in other emergency situations). For further discussion, see Chapter 16.

In taking a history one asks certain questions which are designed to uncover which of these factors play a role. As the therapist further pursues relevant material offered by the patient, common denominators specific to that patient's history emerge. Thus, following up our expectations simultaneously helps us define the patient's pathology. For example, if late in life a patient suffers from a pathological grief reaction or melancholia in response to the loss of a significant other, chances are that he has suffered previous severe loss or losses which make him more vulnerable to later losses. One would, thus, take a history with the possibility of early traumas in mind.

It bears repeating that assessment of psychopathology must not only include conventional genetic and dynamic formulations, but, in order to better define treatment and treatability, be extended to include an appreciation of probable biological givens and predispositions, as well as acute or chronic physiological disturbances that may be subclinical. In gathering these data the family history and medical history (including the results of a recent physical examination) obviously play a crucial role.

Most clinicians are fairly facile with genetic and dynamic formulations. Genetic (biological) limitations and organic problems, if given consideration, can readily be ruled out, and painful surprises avoided. However, a careful ego function assessment, that is, a profile of the adaptive mechanisms critical in negotiating the vicissitudes of life and analytic/psychotherapeutic process, is especially useful, if not critical, to the clinician in *understanding* the patient and in *planning* the therapy. Having a picture of the patient's assets and liabilities, which demonstrates on what level he functions in different areas, provides a key to predicting how he will react to or deal with problems and crises.

Which ego functions are necessary *and* sufficient to effect therapeutic change, of any degree, and what technical variations must be contemplated in order to compensate in those individuals who have deficits and are less than optimal for classical analysis but, given the broad scope of psychoanalysis and psychotherapy currently, are likely to enter into these kinds of therapies? Classically, analysis is concerned with understanding our apperceptive distortions and their effects on our contemporary living in terms of what happened in the past. If the patient has ego deficits, however, then additional forms of therapy are indicated (see Chapter 3). A careful assessment of ego functions will permit anticipation of treatability and of crises and problems likely to occur as a result of poor self-boundaries, depersonalization, etc.

Ego function assessment will provide the basis for a clear conceptualization of the assets which can be utilized and the liabilities which may create problems in the course of treatment. Such assessment permits the therapist to plan the optimum therapeutic strategies and tactics to be employed in the ongoing therapeutic work and in dealing with special crises which may arise.

Making an adequate ego function assessment or profile need not be forbidding. A simple list of functions, such as in Table 1, and a few notes jotted down as one proceeds through an ordinary psychiatric intake interview will provide a good rating. A profile as provided for in Figure 1 will offer graphic clarity.

An example of the use of Ego Function in Psychoanalysis may be found in a brief discussion of two patients.*

Both patients were evaluated at the beginning of analysis using the EFA method (see Figures 2 and 3).

Both patients have undergone periods of crisis, depending on vicissitudes in environmental stress and the analytic work. For example, Patient A went through a suicidal period shortly after the

---

* From "Ego Function Assessment of the Psychoanalytic Process," by Vernon Sharp, M.D. and Leopold Bellak, M.D., *The Psychoanalytic Quarterly*, Vol. XLVII: 52-72, 1978, by permission of the authors and *The Psychoanalytic Quarterly*.

TABLE 1

Ego Functions and Their Components

Ego Function	Components	Ego Function	Components
1. Reality testing	Distinction between inner and outer stimuli Accuracy of perception Reflective awareness and inner reality testing	7. Adaptive regression in the service of the ego	Regressive relaxation of cognitive acuity New configurations
2. Judgment	Anticipation of consequences Manifestation of this anticipation in behavior Emotional appropriateness of this anticipation	8. Defensive functioning	Weakness or obtrusiveness of defenses Success and failure of defenses
3. Sense of reality	Extent of derealization Extent of depersonalization Self-identity and self-esteem Clarity of boundaries between self and world	9. Stimulus barrier	Threshold for stimuli Effectiveness of management of excessive stimulus input
4. Regulation and control of drives, affects, and impulses	Directness of impulse expression Effectiveness of delay mechanisms	10. Autonomous functioning	Degree of freedom from impairment of primary autonomy apparatuses Degree of freedom from impairment of secondary autonomy
5. Object relations	Degree and kind of relatedness Primitiveness (narcissistic, attachment, or symbiotic-object choices) Degree to which others are perceived independently of oneself Object constancy	11. Synthetic-integrative functioning	Degree of reconciliation of incongruities Degree of active relating together of events
		12. Mastery-competence	Competence (how well the subject actually performs in relation to his existing capacity to interact with and actively master and affect his environment) The subjective role (subject's feeling of competence with

| 6. Thought processes | Memory, concentration, and attention
Ability to conceptualize
Primary-secondary process | respect to actively mastering and affecting his environment)
The degree of discrepancy between the other two components (i.e., between actual competence and sense of competence) |

From Bellak, Hurvich & Gediman, 1973. Copyright © 1973, by C. P. S., Inc. Reprinted by permission of John Wiley & Sons, Inc.

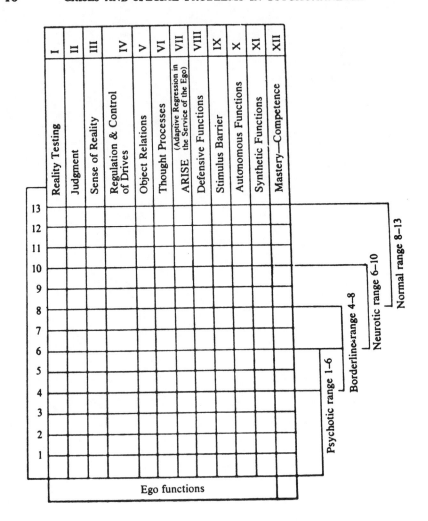

FIGURE 1. Ego Function Profile

From Bellak, Hurvich & Gediman, 1973. Copyright © 1973, by C.P.S., Inc. Reprinted by permission of John Wiley & Sons, Inc.

third anniversary of her mother's death. During this time, conflicts over dependent needs were in the forefront of the analysis, and her self-esteem was at a profoundly low ebb. On one occasion, she became

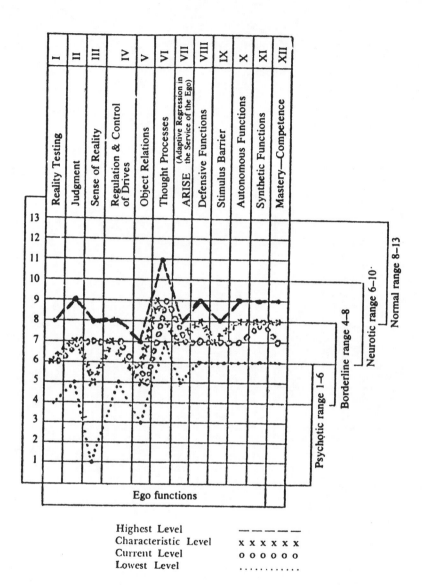

FIGURE 2. Patient A. Onset of Analysis

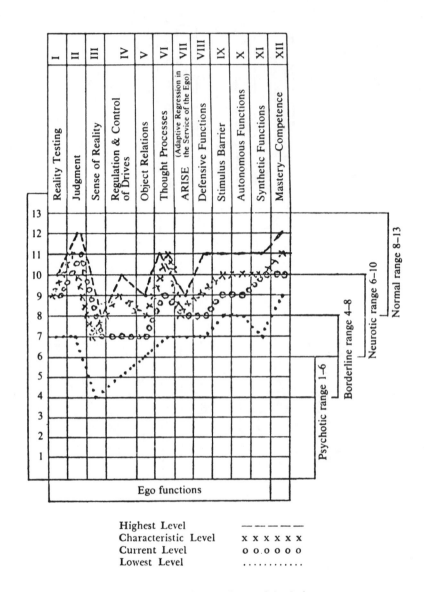

Highest Level   — — — — —
Characteristic Level   x x x x x x
Current Level   o o.o o o o
Lowest Level   . . . .

FIGURE 3. Patient B. Onset of Analysis

suicidal following an hour in which her anger over the analyst's fees began to emerge but was not sufficiently worked through because of an intervening weekend. At the same time, her confused relationships with several young men had taken a turn for the worse, and she had recently been promoted to a position of increased responsibility at her job, a change about which she was ambivalent. The regressive movement of her ego functions under the combined pressures of internal conflict and external stress can be seen in Figure 4.

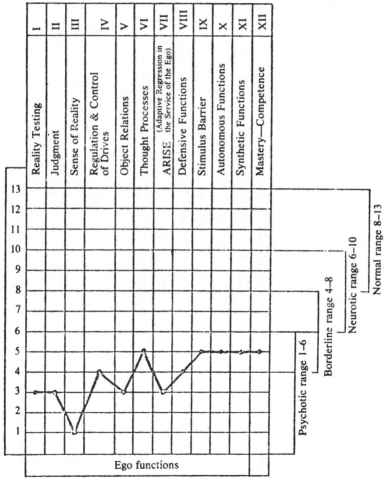

FIGURE 4. Patient A. Rating during a Suicidal Crisis

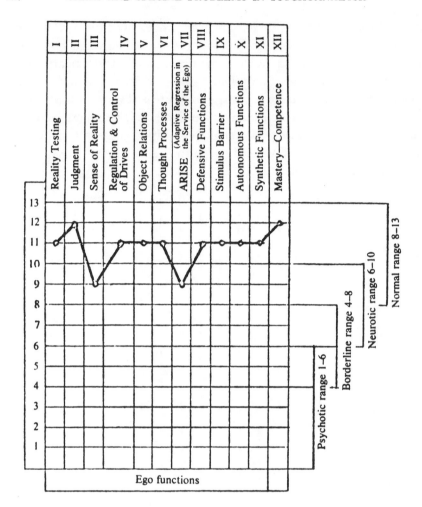

FIGURE 5. Patient B. Rating during a Positive Transference Episode

patient B during an episode of especially strong positive transference.

Having the scheme of ego functions clearly in mind was helpful to the supervised therapist in assessing his countertransference responses during such stormy periods in the course of treatment. In this instance, the trainee was able to correlate the precise changes in the patient's manifest anxiety and altered ego functions with his own perceived anxiety, altered perceptiveness, and therapeutic effectiveness, a process which was quite valuable in the supervision. The systematic use of EFA's in the training of analysts and other therapists has yet to be explored.

Figure 5 illustrates an increase in the ego functioning capacity of This event occurred six months after the analysis had begun. The patient had received a substantial raise in salary and for the first time in his life felt financially secure. However, he was experiencing great pressure to terminate the analysis. He was profoundly doubtful about his work and about his relationships with women and with his male superiors; he wished to withdraw from them all because he felt dangerously overinvolved. Underlying these currents of feeling was an increased sense of comfort and closeness with the therapist, which was being vigorously denied. In spite of his previous accomplishments in the analytic work and his improved financial status, he professed an inability to pay for further treatment, claiming it was an unbearable financial burden. In addition, he felt frustrated in the analysis and was deeply resistant to free associating.

Nevertheless, as work continued over several sessions, he began to perceive his pervasive distancing in all previous relationships, his fears of emotional closeness and terror of abandonment, and finally his sense of never having experienced secure parenting, only a succession of "guardians," from whom he felt no direction or depth of commitment.

3. Ego Function Assessment and Suitability for Psychoanalysis and Psychoanalytic Therapy

The importance of ascertaining the suitability of a patient for analytic therapy and anticipating likely difficulties in the course of it has been stressed earlier.

Ego function assessment for this particular purpose, i.e., for analyzability and possible vicissitudes, can be especially useful. It is merely necessary to keep the 12 ego functions in mind throughout the interview, with particular attention to the implications for the therapeutic process (Bellak & Meyers, 1975).

REALITY TESTING

Important components of reality testing include the intrapersonal and interpersonal validation of perceptions. This is largely a cognitive

Chapter 3 draws on material from an article on "Ego Function Assessment and Analysability," by Leopold Bellak, M.D. and Barnett Meyers, M.D. *The International Review of Psycho-Analysis,* Vol. 2, Part 4, 1975, and a paper by Vernon Sharp, M.D. and Leopold Bellak, M.D. "Ego Function Assessment of the Psychoanalytic Process," *The Psychoanalytic Quarterly,* Vol. XLVII:52-72, 1978.

Both, of course, are predicated on earlier research reported in Bellak, Hurvich and Gediman, *Ego Functions in Schizophrenics, Neurotics, and Normals.* New York: John Wiley & Sons, 1973, and other publications of the author.

The help of all these colleagues and their permission to use the material from these previous publications are herewith gratefully acknowledged.

testing process. Intrapersonal validation refers to the check of data perceived from one sense against that perceived by others, as is lacking in hallucinations. Interpersonal validation involves the comparison of one's own perceptions with those of others, as is lacking in delusions. Any idiosyncratic beliefs that become evident in the consultation must be thoroughly examined with regard to the patient's capacity to test and validate them.

Another principal component is inner reality testing: The analytic process works through an increasing focus on understanding internal reality. It requires a shift of attention from external to internal without losing the capacity to separate the two. The patient is expected to become increasingly aware of how external perceptions are influenced by internal states. The depth and accuracy of internal perceptiveness are related to what we call "psychologic mindedness." Impaired defensive functioning, as manifested by excessive use of denial or projected-introjective mechanisms, limits this perceptiveness and thereby limits the analytic results. Here, as elsewhere, we have to keep in mind the interrelationships of different ego functions, and how strengths or weaknesses of one influence others.

Reality testing is integral to other aspects of the analytic process. Bellak's (1961) conception of "the oscillating function of the ego" can be considered as a "macrofunction," contributed by both adaptive regression and reality testing. The adaptive regression allows for the suspension of secondary process, ensuing free association, and the emergence of previously unconscious material, while the observing reality testing function is required for the recognition and understanding of external and internal reality based on the data of the association.

Reality testing is also critical to the understanding and working through of the transference. At appropriate times the analysand must be able to distinguish internally from externally derived perceptions of the analyst. The regression that produces transference distortions must also be largely reversible at the end of the analysis so that functioning can resume in the patient's daily reality. Borderline and psychotic patients often continue to respond to the internal stimulation of the transference to the point where excessive and unmanageable acting-out ensues. It is thus apparent that a parameter to be used in analyzing patients with deficient reality testing is the modulation of the developing transference by the analyst. Rapid clarification and interpretation of severely distorted transference phenomena become indicated.

JUDGMENT

The analyst must appraise the patient's judgment regarding the analysis itself. How realistic are the patient's expectations or goals? How well does the patient appreciate the type of financial, geographic and temporal commitments that are being made? How well can the patient undergo the voluntary "suspension of disbelief" which relates to the acceptance and awareness of the "as if" (Tarachow, 1963) nature of the transferential relationship? It is such a faculty which permits, for example, the appreciation of and identification with theatrical drama without involvement to the point of running on to the stage to join the performance. Despite the regressive forces inherent in the analysis, a reserve of the function of judgment is necessary for the patient to synchronize the inner and outer realities of the analytic situation and thereby to respond accordingly.

Another significant aspect of judgment is its role in acting-out. Patients with impaired judgment can be expected to act out in a socially inappropriate and perhaps harmful way. The consultation should evaluate judgment demonstrated by the behavior a patient utilized to resolve past conflictual situations. Similar behavior can be expected to be acted out during the analysis. In such cases the analyst may have to supplement the patient's deficiencies in judgment with the analyst's own awareness of the consequences of intended behavior. This awareness can then become signal awareness for the patient at times when self-harming behavior would otherwise be imminent. (See also Regulation and Control of Drives, Affects and Impulses.)

SENSE OF REALITY

The degree of significance of disturbances in the sense of reality in assessing analyzability has yet to be clearly ascertained. Nevertheless, defects here speak for an overall problem with what Beres (1956) and

Frosch (1964) have described as "the relationship to reality." Patients who give a history of responding to stress by regressively losing ego boundaries with resultant perceptual distortions will presumably have this difficulty in the analysis. A particular difficulty could ensue in the transference where severe transference distortions occurring under the influence of a regressive refusion with the analyst could result in an unmanageable "transference psychosis." It is probable that parameters have to be introduced into the analysis of patients with severe defects in this function to maintain the existence of an observing ego, the working alliance and the patient's ability to test his reality. One such parameter is the analyst's "lending" his ego to help the analysand perceive reality at times when it seems irretrievable.

Another parameter is the substitution of face-to-face sessions for the use of the couch. This becomes necessary for patients in whom disturbances in sense of reality readily produce depersonalized or derealized states associated with such severe anxiety that analysis of the state becomes impossible.

The use of the couch need not be an all-or-none proposition. The patient may be able to use the couch most of the time, but may need to sit up when feelings of depersonalization or derealization emerge to a disturbing degree. When the relevant problems are analyzed, the patient is usually able to return to the couch (Sharp & Bellak, 1978).

REGULATION AND CONTROL OF DRIVES, AFFECTS AND IMPULSES

Impaired regulation of drives is directly related to a tendency towards acting-out. Acting-out becomes a too easily used means of remembering and, as such, an alternative to analyzing and understanding conflicts *within* the analysis. Thus, in order for the analysis to progress, the frustration of not acting out transference wishes must be tolerated. The interpretation of the wishes within the analysis then results in a second loss and resultant frustration. As Tarachow (1963) points out, all transference interpretations result in a loss in that the patient must reaccept the "as if" transference quality of the relationship. It is a difficult set of steps for the analysand to (a) first feel the impulses, (b) then renounce the gratification offered by acting them out, (c) bring the wishes into the analysis, (d) accept the loss that results from interpretation, and (e) use the interpretation to synthesize a new understanding and relinquish old object wishes.

Bellak (1963), in describing the psychology of acting-out, suggests a number of points in its treatment, some of which are directly relevant here: Even at the beginning of the analysis it can be important to predict for patients who appear to have a tendency to act out that this is likely to arise, including their desire to interrupt the analysis. They may do this seemingly for external reasons or because of hostile feelings towards the analyst. It may be appropriate in the initial interviews, or early in the analysis, to point out to the patients the situations in which they are especially likely to act out and thus to increase their signal awareness. In this way an important therapeutic alliance can be established which may make the difference between a successful and an unsuccessful analysis.

Patients who give historical evidence of requiring immediate relief from anxiety or depression have analytic difficulties in this area. These are often the same patients who have histories of overstimulation and have constitutional or experiential deficiencies in stimulus barrier.

Patients who evidence deficient drive regulation combined with overtly gratifying symptomatology present particular problems. These relate to some of the difficulties encountered in the treatment of drug abuse and the perversions.

A parameter to be considered in dealing with weaknesses in this function is the addition of medication at times when excessive anxiety combined with deficient affect modulation has a particularly disorganizing effect. The amount and duration of such psychopharmacologic interventions must be carefully monitored so as to allow for an optimal affect as well as cognitive functioning level consistent with the analytic work.

OBJECT RELATIONS

Failures in the development of object relations have particular effects upon an analysis. Failure to differentiate self from object is the distinguishing characteristic of the psychoses, but in a more subtle form is also a manifestation of narcissistic personality disorders. In these narcissistic non-psychotic disturbances, the separation of internal self and object representations has occurred, and consequently the individual can distinguish internal from external reality (reality test). However, due to both incomplete mastery of separation and unresolved wishes for refusion, the narcissistic patient is liable to transiently *feel* external objects as extensions of the self. The result, in both psychosis and narcissistic disturbance, is that within the analysis, losses resulting from absence, silence, vacation and transference interpretations lead to a severe anxiety that recapitulates infantile separation anxiety.

Disturbances in object relations can lead to transference resistance or resistance to transference. In the former, the analyst is perceived and maintained as the projection of an all good idealized "real" object. Analysis of this fusion would lead to a profound narcissistic loss. In the latter, the analyst is perceived as a powerful threatening figure via projective identification and such a transference makes a working alliance impossible. The severe forms of disturbance are classically seen in narcissistic and borderline conditions.

Kohut (1971) has specifically described the vicissitudes in object relations of the patient with a narcissistic character disorder and the analytic modifications and technical measures necessary to plan on. Kernberg (1968) has discussed parameters that may become necessary during the analysis of both narcissistic and borderline disturbances. Jacobson (1971), in turn, has especially described the psychodynamics of the transference relationship of the severely depressed patient. In patients described by these authors, it is important to be fully aware of all the factors that are likely to manifest themselves as problems of analyzability at the earliest possible opportunity. In many cases the analyst must decide as to the feasibility of restructuring infantile object representations, as opposed to a less classical approach that would aim at internalizing a new object by identification with the analyst. Naturally, this is never an all-or-none proposition.

Less severely distorted object relations are seen in neurotic disorders and, prototypically, in the transference neurosis. It is through the transference that we have most direct access to an examination of how internalized mental representations from childhood influence current perceptions and object relations. This can be contrasted to the hypothetic optimal level of object relatedness in which the perception of external objects remains constant regardless of affectual or instinctual changes. It is of note that in order for an analysis to take place there must be a regression in just this area. The patient must regress from his own optimal level of object relatedness in order to develop the transference distortions essential for an analysis. The limiting factor must be the level of individuation already achieved so that the transference distortions do not become symbiotic refusions or do not require the use of intransigent splitting, denial, idealization, or other primitive defenses that make the transference unanalyzable.

Classical theory of analyzability has been somewhat divergent from actual practice. According to the most classical, and undoubtedly most gratifying model of an analysis, interpretation of the defenses leads to the establishment of a transference neurosis. This transference neurosis is not only a renascence of the childhood neurosis, but also the somewhat varying model of the patient's conflicts and problems in general, reproduced like a laboratory preparation in the analytic setting. In this ideal situation, the interpretation of the transference neurosis leads by automatic generalization to a corrective therapeutic restructuring of the personality of the patient via this model. It is as if a calibrator were directly to transfer the learning from the small transference analysis model to the large, life-sized scale of all relationships.

The fact is, however, that a majority of the patients currently seen in western cultures rarely produce a classical transference neurosis unless they suffer from a hysterical disorder, possibly close to a borderline condition. While most patients do not produce a full-blown transference neurosis, they do so to a small extent from time to time throughout the analysis. It would be a mistake to consider a limited ability to produce any kind of transference neurosis as a preclusion to analysis.

THOUGHT PROCESSES

Disturbances in thinking have traditionally been excessively related to schizophrenics. There is evidence that some schizophrenics do not have a thought disorder and some non-schizophrenics do (Bellak et al., 1973).

Especially noteworthy is an increasing awareness that mild neurological conditions, which in childhood probably manifested themselves as dyslexia or other learning disabilities with some soft neurological signs (minimal brain dysfunction), may also result in thought disorders under the impact of flooding by emotions. (Patients with such conditions not only need to be specifically diagnosed with regard to their analyzability, but they also need, themselves, to understand the origin of their disorder.) Such patients may at times sound psychotic to themselves and others. A decreased tendency to be flooded by neurotic emotions will decrease their tendency towards confused thinking. At the same time, awareness and understanding of this tendency are essential. In this case a neurological deficit contributes to poor control of drives and affects with a consequent disturbance in thinking.

Defects in the thinking process have clearcut effects on the analytic process. Free association requires controlled regression of thought processes. The ego must be capable of oscillating in such a way that secondary process thought can take over to perceive and understand primary process material that has emerged. The analysand must be able to use attention, concentration, memory and concept formation in order to be aware of his associations, be capable of recalling them and, finally, be able to decipher themes and form concepts regarding his internal reality. *The capacity to think syllogistically is relevant here.* The analyst's use of, and the patient's understanding of syllogisms is critical to interpretation and insight.

ADAPTIVE REGRESSION IN THE SERVICE OF THE EGO

As Kris (1952) and others have pointed out, adaptive regression is an essential aspect of the creative act and thus has a critical role in the analytic process. This function, firstly, allows for the relaxation of cognitive acuity and secondary process modes of thought to permit the emergence of more mobile preconscious and unconscious ideation and, secondly, involves the ego's capacity to interrupt and reverse the regression and return to secondary process thought. The third aspect of this function is the ego's capacity to utilize the regression adaptively by inducing new configurations and creative integrations.

Defects in any of the aspects of adaptive regression result in specific difficulties in the analysis.

The obsessive-compulsive personality will have great difficulty suspending secondary process thought because of the anxiety produced by affects, instincts and the fluidity of cathexes. His thinking will remain concrete. This same anxiety about the unknown (unconscious) will impair such a patient's ability to form creative and new integrations adaptively. The schizophrenic and borderline patients can readily regress to primary process modes of thought but have difficulties reversing the process. The anxiety resulting from the loss of control of the thinking process in such patients impedes the adaptive utilization of the regression as well.

The initial interview is an invaluable tool here. Can the patient fantasize? Is he aware of his dreams and how does he respond to them? Is the patient capable of the regressions called for in the appreciation of art, sex or humor, or are they felt as threatening and ego-alien? Alternatively, does the patient regress "too readily" and not in the service of the ego? Does the patient evidence primary process thought in a structured interview? Is there a history of fantasies interrupting intended concentration in a disabling fashion or of a preoccupation with and "being carried away by" fantasies?

Regarding the second phase of the oscillating process, the interviewer can investigate whether the patient has been able to use discoveries from dreams, fantasies or other regressed states for planned or creative actions. How does he go about problem-solving? Does he discover imaginative solutions via ego regression or can he only approach solutions by rote learning?

Finally, the question arises as to how smoothly the patient can make the transition from the regression to control. Can the ego use regression and its controls in a complementary fashion that can lead to adaptation? A microcosm of this occurs in the consultation itself where the patient relinquishes usual inhibitions to speak of emotionally charged anxiety-producing material. The interview must attend to how the patient responds to this regression and to the thoughts it evokes. A patient who is able to regress in a limited fashion, who finds this pleasurable and, most importantly, a patient who can use the consultation to form limited yet *new* understandings about the self creatively, is demonstrating evidence for a positive prognosis—at least in regard to this ego function's contribution to the outcome of the analysis.

In many cases the analyst can help the patient modulate the degree of regression during an hour so as to achieve an optimal regressive level for adaptive utilization. In some patients medication can be considered which might decrease the effect of anxiety on the oscillating function. Excessive and maladaptive regression can be interrupted by the analyst's increased activity or by rhe temporary substitution of face-to-face sessions for the couch.

DEFENSIVE FUNCTIONING

We must consider how deficits here can be identified during the initial consultations and what parameters are available for dealing with such deficits during the course of the analysis.

Incapacitating dysphoria will have a disruptive effect. Severe depression will result in retardation of thought and associations, as well as a general impairment of cognition. Excessive anxiety has an obvious disorganizing effect. Patients presenting such severe affective symptoms are often suffering from a failure of repression and necessitate, at least initially, a more "supportive" psychotherapeutic approach. The use of psychoanalysis can be reconsidered later, but even then, the introduction of parameters that would help to bind dysphoria might be required.

Patients who bind their dysphoria but at the cost of maladaptation present the converse problem. The lack of anxiety and depression decreases the motivation towards analysis. The alloplastic tendency lends itself to acting-out. In the obsessive-compulsive the defenses of isolation and intellectualization, by preventing the emergence of affects, are mitigating against the development, awareness and understanding of transference feelings. Patients suffering from perversions or psychosomatic illnesses, because of the rapid discharge of affect inherent in their conditions, can be expected to present similar difficulties.

The more punitive defenses produce the greatest reality distortions and are therefore the most difficult to analyze. A patient whose presentation reveals an extensive use of denial can be expected to be quite resistant to perceiving, much less analyzing, the disturbing internal reality. The tendency to perceive problems as externally caused is associated with denial and projection and presents similar difficulties. This applies not only to overtly manic or paranoid patients but is also seen in what are often referred to as "acting-out" forms of character disorders. Finally, the borderline patient's tendency to split will be revealed in the consultation by a history of defensive over-idealization or denigration of significant objects. The transference distortions resulting from splitting are often intransigent to analysis (Kernberg, 1967, 1968).

STIMULUS BARRIER

A critical aspect of this function is the individual's ability to regulate the stimulus threshold: One of the coping mechanisms towards stimulation is modulation and selectivity of attentiveness. This screening mechanism allows for adaptive changes in sensitivity to stimulation, thus facilitating periods of heightened acuity, focused concentration and the general filtering out of stimulation necessary for sleep. Other aspects of the expressive component include the degree of cognitive and motoric adaptation to high levels of stimulation versus motoric and cognitive disruption. Persons with a low stimulus threshold plus poor coping mechanisms are easily "overstimulated," leading to impaired sleep habits, concentration, mood and drive regulation, synthetic functioning, etc. It is thus clear that overflow from defects in this function can influence the other ego functions as well.

The ego's capacity to regulate stimulus input plays a critical role in the analytic process. The analytic setting is designed to reduce external stimulation and thereby promote regression and an increased attention to internal phenomena. The patient cooperates in this screening out of external stimulation. Patients with impairments here are easily distracted and such distractions can become a major obstacle to the analysis. The emphasis here is not on the psychic meaning of such distractions, but that some patients lack the ego capacity to adequately screen out adventitious stimulation.

Patients with such impairments often give histories of daily experiences in which sensory overstimulation has led to disorganization. Not being able to cope with the impact of small children or of having to orientate oneself while driving in a new environment are commonplace examples of this.

In this context we want to refer to the too rarely recognized problem of adults who, as children, suffered from a minimal brain dysfunction and may still have, on the one hand, a low stimulus barrier and, on the other hand, some problems in orientation. Sometimes they are actually left-handed or ambidextrous and some have problems of orientation in space—more problems than they are aware of. For example, in instances where there was frequent marital discord because a spouse tended to get lost while driving to some destination, examination revealed that difficulties in telling right from left as part of a minimal brain disorder were responsible for the patient's poor sense of direction.

Another aspect of this is sensitivity to the effects of internal changes. How disorganizing does the consultee find the experience of pain or discomfort, or, in the case of women, premenstrual tension? The analysand must, rather than be overwhelmed by internal stimulation, have the capacity to perceive and utilize such stimulation in the service of self-understanding. Patients with strengths here can more readily understand the relationship between sensations that are perceived and their psychological meaning.

Conversely, the concept of a required minimal stimulation relates to this function. The classical example of deficient stimulation disrupting psychic functioning is in the sensory deprivation syndrome and persons vary in regard to their sensitivity to this. Patients requiring moderate amounts of stimulation to preserve psychic integration can be expected to derealize or have transient psychotic experiences in the sensory deprivation that is inherent to the analytic situation. Such patients may require a well lit room or increased verbal activity by the analyst to prevent such experiences.

A paradigm for the evaluation of stimulus barrier can be how the consultee deals with the task of falling asleep. Is sleep too readily prevented by minimal external stimulation? Conversely, has the lack of stimulation inherent to falling asleep required the use of hypnotic agents or the auxiliary stimulation of the television or radio? The dynamic significances of sleep disturbances are myriad. Nevertheless, a critical element is how well the patient can regulate the stimulus barrier to achieve the level of stimulation necessary for sleep and how this regulatory capacity will facilitate or impede the analysis.

AUTONOMOUS FUNCTIONING

One can conceptualize the autonomous ego functions *as the tools the patient brings* to the therapeutic alliance to accomplish the analytic work. Deficits in these tools can severely limit the amount of work done. This is clearly true when we consider impairments in intelligence, language, memory and attentiveness, and their effects in the analytic process. The same is true for the complex patterns that make up secondary autonomous functions. What acquired intellectual and perceptual skills (which include communication, the ability to symbolize and understand symbols, etc.) does the patient bring to the analysis? To what extent are other major ego functions such as reality testing, judgment and thought processes operating free from conflict? How likely are these functions to regress and in what conflictual areas? A patient who develops severe anxiety with loosened associations when discussing overtly sexual material has such impairment of reality testing, thinking, object relations and his primary functions at such times that the capacity to perceive or understand the difficulties is lost.

We can always anticipate a degree of regressive instinctualization of what had previously been autonomous functions during the course of an analysis. What we must consider are the autonomous starting points and the autonomous reserves the patient will maintain. This will help decide the kind and degree of effort and equipment the patient has available for the analysis. Persons who already suffer from inability to perform simple work habits or intellectual tasks, for whom such tasks now seem a burden and who have lost the ability to concentrate or communicate clearly, are usually not ready to start an analysis. In such cases a preparatory course of therapy is often indicated, followed by a reassessment to determine the capacities of autonomous functions to contribute to and withstand the rigors of an analysis.

SYNTHETIC-INTEGRATIVE FUNCTION

As Beres (1956) has pointed out, the synthetic function's activity is ubiquitous in human thought and action. It works so closely with other functions that its examination in isolation is nearly impossible. Nevertheless, the critical nature of this function's contribution to the analytic process makes such a dissection and investigation imperative. Without adequate synthetic integrative functioning, the reductive dissective aspects of the psychoanalytic process would lead to dissolution and psychosis rather than re-synthesis and ego growth.

The associative process by which the connections occur also depends heavily on this function. Without it, the second phase of the oscillating function does not occur and free association becomes the loosened autistic associative process of the schizophrenic. The synthetic function allows for the linkage of initially casual associative data in order to arrive at causal and dynamic themes and understanding.

The psychoanalytic process is itself a dissociative experience: The patient is asked to observe himself and report on himself (Bellak, 1961). This involves both phases of the oscillating function, i.e., adaptive regression followed by synthesis. In some people with a poor synthetic function, the analytic process actually increases a tendency towards pathological dissociation. Having previously been self-ob-

serving in an unskilled way, they now substitute analytic self-observation. In the absence of a sufficient ego synthetic function, they are
unable to utilize interpretations in a constructive way. They are primarily the people who do well intellectually, but are unable to
integrate and synthesize the experience emotionally into the necessary gestalt that, indeed, is ultimately responsible for a restructuring
of the personality. For that reason, insufficient synthetic function to
utilize insight is a contraindication to analysis and calls for psychotherapy with limited associating, limited self-observing and other
forms of intervention. Very often people who have been unsuccessfully
analyzed, with a specific complaint of constant self-analysis and no
symptom resolution, need postanalytic psychotherapy, specifically to
undo the dissociative aspects of analysis.

Appraisal of this function during initial interviews should include
evaluation of the frequency and severity of dissociative states. How
well does the patient integrate affects with thoughts? How well has
the patient been able to sort out excessive stimulation by specifically
synthesizing the various stimuli to arrive at an understanding of
the specific situation? Patients with neurologic defects, particularly
involving minimal brain dysfunction, may present difficulties here.

One parameter that can be introduced into the analysis of some
patients would be the analyst's lending his own synthesizing function
to the patient. The analyst could thus concretely review and synthesize significant elements of the session. The analyst would have
to help the patient integrate the affective state and the thought content. The hoped for result would be a strengthening of the patient's
own integrative function so that the patient could then carry out
such processes independently.

MASTERY-COMPETENCE

The mastery we are considering here is of the analytic task. In
essence, we are considering how well an individual utilizes the
analytic insights to work through and resolve conflicts. Difficulties
with this late step in the analytic course explain a difference between

patients who understand the infantile origins of their conflicts while continuing neurotic patterns, and patients who, by working through conflicts, become free to achieve behavioral and characterologic changes.

The preanalysis evaluation must assess this function and consider the potential analysand's sense of competency and its relation to actual achievement. Is the patient unrealistically grandiose or unduly pessimistic? Does he "underachieve" and why?

Patients with character traits marked by strong passive and/or masochistic wishes become problematic here. The literature has considered these issues and the related topic of the negative therapeutic reaction (Freud, 1937). The resistances that develop in such patients are usually considered in terms of their psychodynamic origins or manifestations in the transference. We are not minimizing such issues but are rather focusing on another perspective through which to view them: Masochistic and passive-dependent character pathology leads to impairment of the ego's functioning, specifically in its capacity to achieve mastery and competence. We would predict that without a certain resource level of this function, regardless of the strengths of the other functions, a weakness in the so-called *"analytic utilization factor"* results in a consequent limitation on the potential analytic achievement. A corollary to this is that some relatively more disturbed patients who bring a particularly strong utilization factor to the analysis, as evidenced by a history of past environmental masteries, may be surprisingly good candidates for analysis.

In the systematic evaluation of ego functions for the assessment of analyzability, superego factors and, to some extent, drive factors have not been considered. Similarly, reality factors, specific maturational phase or general life situation, intelligence, various handicaps such as speech difficulties, hearing difficulties, congruence or incongruence of a given patient with a given psychoanalyst were also not discussed. In no way should the limitation of the present discussion be construed as a willingness or suggestion that factors other than ego function assessment should be ignored or considered unimportant, or even less important.

REFERENCES

BELLAK, L. Free association: Conceptual and clinical aspects. *Int. J. Psycho-Anal.*, 42, 9-20, 1961.

BELLAK, L. Acting out: Some conceptual and therapeutic considerations. *Amer. J. Psychother.*, 17, 375-389, 1963.

BELLAK, L., HURVICH, M., & GEDIMAN, H. *Ego Functions in Schizophrenics, Neurotics, and Normals.* New York: John Wiley & Sons, 1973.

BELLAK, L. & MEYERS, B. Ego function assessment and analysability. *The International Review of Psycho-Analysis*, Vol. 2, 413-427, 1975.

BERES, D. Ego deviation and the concept of schizophrenia. *Psychoanal. Study Child*, 2, 164-235, 1956.

FREUD, S. (1937). Analysis terminable and interminable. *Standard Edition of Complete Psychological Works of Sigmund Freud*, Vol. 23. London: Hogarth.

FROSCH, J. The psychotic character: Clinical psychiatric considerations. *Psychiat. Q.*, 38, 81-96, 1964.

JACOBSON, E. *Depression: Comparative Studies of Normal, Neurotic, and Psychotic Conditions.* New York: Int. Univ. Press, 1971.

KERNBERG, O. Borderline personality organization. *J. Am. Psychoanal. Assn.*, 15, 641-685, 1967.

KERNBERG, O. The treatment of patients with borderline personality organization. *Int. J. Psycho-Anal.*, 49, 600-619, 1968.

KOHUT, H. *The Analysis of the Self.* New York: Int. Univ. Press, 1971.

KRIS, E. *Psychoanalytic Explorations in Art.* New York: Int. Univ. Press, 1952.

SHARP, V. & BELLAK, L. Ego function assessment of the psychoanalytic process. *The Psychoanalytic Quarterly*, Vol. XLVII: 52-72, 1978.

TARACHOW, S. *An Introduction to Psychotherapy.* New York: Int. Univ. Press, 1963.

4. The Armamentarium

Patients may initially present themselves in a crisis. Even if psychoanalysis may be planned for eventually, emergency psychotherapy may be a necessary forerunner as an enabling condition for later long-term therapy. Other patients present in a relatively stable condition and enter a crisis in response to extrinsic circumstances or to some event intrinsic to the therapeutic process.

If patients *present in a crisis,* one must synthesize a rational treatment plan. Synthesizing a rational treatment plan based on the mass of information culled in the careful Anamnesis and Assessment discussed in Chapter 2 often leaves the clinician on the firing line. Faced with the broad spectrum of clinical problems and crises presenting today, he may well ask himself, "What should I do? What can I do? What may I do?" Confronted with the more problematical patient, one often hears the lament, "This is not a good patient." This cry really seems to be an expression of the frustration experienced by rigidly trained traditional clinicians with a limited, that is, tightly circumscribed, treatment approach. It is also an expression of their reticence to consider and explore alternatives or modifications of approach even when, unfortunately for the patient, the standard treatment does not fit the disease. The position of the "ideal" therapist who "knows everything and does as little as possible" is a stance which can be approximated with some patients, and the elusive, but incisive, cathartic interpretation can indeed be savored on occasion.

41

But more likely, the therapist in general practice today will not have the luxury of adhering rigidly and exclusively to this approach. If he wishes to be at all practical, he ought to be prepared to have at his disposal and to skillfully employ, as needed, a wide range of therapeutic interventions, including not only the conventional verbal modes, but also environmental manipulations and the use of family and community resources, auxiliary medical services, and psychopharmacology. He must be able to select from his armamentarium the appropriate instrument(s) for the therapeutic task at hand, whether this be classical analysis, dealing with a special problem, or crisis intervention.

Keeping in mind the overall picture, that is, our understanding of the main constellation of the patient's personality structure provided by the anamnesis and assessment, the clinician will then be able to select the best area, sequence, and method of intervention, provided he is thoroughly familiar with various treatment approaches and has developed facility in carrying them out. Our theoretical equipment (our equivalents of anatomy, physiology, pathology, and *therapeutics*) provides a preconceived notion of what constitutes *appropriate intervention* in most situations. For this reason, the clinician need not feel he is alone and starting from scratch, as is wont to happen in this profession, where many of us work in relative isolation.

For example, let us consider treatment of a depression: The anamnesis has revealed prior experiences with loss, difficulties with self-esteem regulation, problems with intra-aggression or other dynamic considerations; an ego assessment has provided you with information regarding adaptive assets and liabilities. You may choose in one case a cathartic interpretation. However, in another case, where conflict around aggression is great and impulse controls are poor, such an interpretation is likely to create even more overwhelming anxiety. Therefore, one would preferably select a more supportive and ego-building intervention. In cases where ego deficits are extreme, one might also call into service external supports such as the family and social/environmental manipulations, including hospitalization. If, in addition, careful assessment of personal and family history has indicated biological underpinnings of a particular disorder, then, of course, commensurate modes of treatment should be instituted. Specific interventions such as these constitute knowing where to help and being equipped to do it.

The specificity of the intervention is all important. Therefore, first let us consider in a general way the range of interventions that ought to be available to the clinician and with which he ought to have a working facility when faced with designing an initial treatment *plan*, or when faced with a special problem or crisis in the course of treatment. Being well-versed in numerous and various interventions permits the clinician to formulate a notion of which types of intervention(s) would be most effective in a particular case and which could lead to trouble. Devising a treatment plan in accordance with a dynamic view of the patient is an exercise which in itself can further clarify the therapist's conceptualization of his patient.

If crises arise *in the course of treatment,* it is important to relate them to intercurrent events of external or internal nature. Since the patient is often unaware of the nature of the precipitating event, careful reconstruction of external events in the patient's life is necessary. At the same time, a clear conceptualization of the dynamic events of the preceding therapeutic sessions is necessary. The essential task is *to establish continuity where there is discontinuity*—the basic contribution of psychotherapy.

SOME METHODS OF INTERVENTION IN CRISIS SITUATION

Interpretation

Interpretation is, of course, the royal road to the unconscious: the finding of common denominators in behavioral, cognitive, affective factors, and of factors common to contemporary and past behavior, and common to contemporary, past and transference reactions. Interpretation is the main avenue for establishing continuity.

Usually, interpretation involves facets which are mostly preconscious for the patient. The step to consciousness is then a relatively small one. Much of psychoanalytic technique is concerned with the slow increase in awareness that makes conflicts, anxieties and inter-actions interpretable.

In crisis situations, the analytic therapist may not be able to wait until some troublesome material reaches preconsciousness. The crisis, in fact, may be related to the unacceptability of the repressed ma-terial. A dramatic interpretation then may take the form of a *cathartic interpretation*—direct translation of unconscious material by the analyst to the patient. The image of the cathartic is illustrative: One expects a sudden rush of affect, experienced in the safe surrounding of the office, capable of being dealt with by support, intellectual clarification and, above all, working-through in the transference of the threatening feelings. This dramatic intervention also elicits pictures of the lancing of an abscess. The pain is acute before, is worse during the lancing, and is followed by the relief of decompression.

Cathartic interpretations are at times especially indicated when acting-out of an unconscious process is clearly a threatening develop-ment.

Catharsis can be an important intervention, although its role is exaggerated in such faddist therapies as primal scream. A common mistake is to believe that catharsis alone will have a therapeutic effect, when the fact is that it is a form of intervention that is rarely suffi-cient by itself.

Mediate catharsis is used to mean expressing emotionally charged propositions for the patient. For example, with a depressed patient with a severe superego and a good deal of aggression, one may say, "Certainly if the foreman had done that to me, I would have kicked him." The therapist is thus expressing sentiments for the patient which might be too strong for his sensitive superego and, by virtue of the therapist's stating them, he takes the superego responsibility. He also conveys to the patient that if an authority such as the ther-apist can permit himself such an aggressive thought, it may not be so unacceptable. Identification and introjection of the therapist as a more benign part of the superego then assume an important role in this part of the therapeutic process.

Another form of indirect or mediate catharsis should be con-sidered: "Of course, a conscientious person like yourself would not permit himself to think this, let alone to do it, but somebody else might certainly feel like killing the son-of-a-bitch." By this statement, the therapist gives the patient a double message: first, the reassurance that he would never lose such control and that, as a matter of fact, he is a person of strict conscience; and second, the idea that, in this instance, such aggressive sentiments are not inappropriate.

Reality Testing

Reality testing is necessary in proportion to how disturbed a patient is and how great a need there is for the therapist to play the role of an auxiliary reality tester, interpreting the patient's distortions of reality and functioning as an auxiliary ego for him.

Drive Repression

Drive repression may be utilized with a patient who feels that he ought to submit to peer pressure—e.g., with regard to promiscuity—but who has reacted or may predictably react to such behavior with panic. For example, in the case of an adolescent girl who feels that she has to engage in a certain amount of promiscuity to have social standing in her high school, the therapist might flatly say that she simply should not engage in sex unless she feels absolutely comfortable and it is an expression of her desire rather than what she thinks is expected. He will then help her to accept that one does not have to be promiscuous to be accepted by one's peers. By this means, the burden is taken off her mind, or, at least, a pause takes place in which she can reconstitute. By selective inattention, one may sometimes discourage some forms of behavior and encourage others, in effect bringing about selective repression in the patient. It must be borne in mind, however, that repression plays a normal role in daily functioning and that insufficient repression is, of course, at least as much a problem as excessive repression.

Sensitization of Signals

Sensitization to signals is concerned with making the patient aware that certain behaviors on his part, whether acting-out or panic, occur when there is a specific dynamic constellation. It may involve nothing more sophisticated than pointing out to a patient that she always has a flare-up with her husband in the two or three days preceding her period.

Education

Education of the above-mentioned patient might involve acquainting her with the facts about sodium retention and irritability and advising her to reduce her salt intake. The therapist might possibly prescribe a mild diuretic and/or sedative for the two or three premenstrual days to help her avoid a serious marital conflict. Education of an adolescent patient, to offer another example, might involve a lesson in the anatomy or physiology involved in sexual functioning if simple ignorance in this area is causing anxiety.

Intellectualization

Intellectualization usually plays a greater role in brief therapy than in traditional longer-term therapies. However, even in psychoanalysis and long-term psychoanalytic psychotherapy, it can sometimes be used to increase the therapeutic alliance. In other cases, with very panicky patients for example, it offers assurance that the therapist has at least an intellectual understanding of the symptom. Transmitting this intellectual understanding to the patient will give him some control over what otherwise seems to be totally disruptive and ego-alien behavior.

Support

Support, in the form of the therapist's acceptance of various feelings expressed by the patient—whether they be aggression, sexuality, or greed—makes it easier for the patient to bear the anxiety associated with these impulses. Making reassuring statements is important at certain times in therapy, but it can never be the sole intervention if one expects to provide something more than just ad hoc help.

Conjoint Sessions and Family Network Therapy

Conjoint sessions and family network therapy are special techniques which cannot be dealt with in detail here, except to say that they may be used in connection with various interventions in a very specific way. The therapist should clearly conceptualize what he wants to cover in a conjoint session and then arrange for that session in order to accomplish the circumscribed goals.

Auxiliary Therapist

At times a patient develops true panic in analysis in response to threatening transference feelings. These are often of either a sexual or an aggressive nature, and often involve fear of passivity as well.

If these are not otherwise readily manageable, it may be advisable to introduce a colleague as temporary auxiliary therapist. The patient will see him or her merely for an analysis of transference feelings towards the primary therapist. At times an auxiliary therapist of the the other sex is especially advisable, for example, in the case of homosexual panic.

An auxiliary therapist may also be useful for the management of acting-out in the transference. The patient in a panic wants to cling. Emergency intervention by the primary therapist might compromise therapeutic neutrality nearly irreparably. The auxiliary therapist can, however, engage in necessary emergency interventions without such danger. The secondary gain which a patient often derives from acting-out in the transference is then also effectively interfered with by shunting him off to an auxiliary therapist.

In the treatment of psychotics, countertransference and anxiety may become so severe for a therapist that sharing the burden with an auxiliary therapist may also be a useful step under these circumstances.

Psychoactive Drugs

Psychoactive drugs, as a form of intervention, appear to aid the therapist in the way anesthesia does the surgeon: They help provide a therapeutic climate in which to work. In therapy, they are often part of the enabling conditions which make it possible to sufficiently control anxiety, disturbed thought processes, or depression so that the patient can remain in the community and continue with psychotherapy, which otherwise might be extremely difficult or impossible for him. Approach-anxiety with regard to conflictual material will often keep a patient from facing certain insights. In such instances, anxiolytic drugs are useful in decreasing approach-anxiety, at least enough so that the patient is willing to deal with his problems in therapy. In those patients with thought disorders, phenothiazines may greatly facilitate interaction in the short run or help to control impulses which may otherwise prove to be too disruptive. The main proposition concerning the usefulness of drugs in connection with psychotherapy is that one use enough medication to facilitate therapy but not so much as to interfere with motivation for further therapeutic work or cloud the cognitive processes, making it impossible for the patient to participate in the psychotherapeutic process.

5. Special Interventions for Specific Ego Function Deficits

THE CHOICE OF SOME STRUCTURAL INTERVENTIONS

Using the same 12 ego functions previously discussed in Chapter 3, the following considerations are useful to keep in mind for the management of serious disturbances.

1) TREATMENT OF DISTURBANCES OF REALITY TESTING

Whatever the severity of disturbance of reality testing, the therapist's role is to a certain extent that of an *auxiliary ego*.

If the disturbance of reality testing is severe (e.g., if the patient lives primarily in a world of delusions and hallucinations), a number of preliminary steps are necessary: *entering into the patient's world;* establishing understanding on a *primary-process level;* gaining the *patient's confidence.* Letting the patient know that he is being understood decreases his secondary terror (about his strange world) and makes possible some bridging of the gap between the psychotic world and reality.

Interpretation of some of the patient's distortions is then possible. There may be cathartic interpretations of feared drive impulses (best

49

exemplified by John Rosen's (1953) technique), of defenses or of the superego factors, judiciously paced.

It may be a necessary part of therapy to include *sensitizing the patient* to *the perception of inner reality*—for example, getting him to recognize anger or anxiety before they are translated into major or minor projections. *Prediction* of possible distortion of emerging events will play a major role in the patient's avoiding the distortion and helping him recognize traumatic situations. This holds true particularly for defects in judgment, as seen in various degrees of acting-out.

Education may play a role if some of the defects in reality testing are exacerbated by inadequate *information* (e.g., a fear of becoming pregnant from a kiss).

Drugs may play a major role in the control of *excess drives* responsible for the distortion of *reality*. Psychotropic drugs, for example, can improve reality testing indirectly, and the phenothiazines may have an effect on the synthetic function, thereby improving the quality of thinking and, in turn, reality testing.

Group psychotherapy, like a rehabilitation-workshop setting, may provide *feedback for reality testing*: If the patient behaves or talks unrealistically, the group or workshop personnel will let him know about it. Inasmuch as faulty reality testing in such settings does not lead to dire consequences but to therapeutic intervention, they are "settings of self-correcting reality."

Id and superego are actively involved in reality testing. For instance, unrealistic *guilt feelings* may be at the root of self-harming, masochistic behavior. *Excessive sexual push* (e.g., in involutional disorders) may lead specifically to grossly sexual delusions and hallucinations. In such cases, the whole therapeutic armamentarium, from interpretations designed to achieve insight to drug therapy, is appropriate in the service of improved reality testing.

2) TREATMENT OF DISTURBANCES OF JUDGMENT

It is entirely possible to be able to test reality adequately and yet be *insufficiently aware of the probable consequences of ill-considered* action. A common example of such a situation is acting-out, which spans normal, neurotic, and psychotic behavior. Persons given to acting-out can, if queried about the details of reality, offer perfectly accurate accounts. Because of the impulses motivating their behavior, however, they engage in acts which, in everyone else's eyes, demonstrate poor judgment. Even eminent scientists and outstanding statesmen make such mistakes in judgment. A scientist of great repute, who certainly must ordinarily have excellent judgment, nearly came to grief when he and his son, neither of whom could swim, went sailing on the ocean. A highly placed government figure of ascetic personality, in accepting a relatively minor gift, ruined his career with a presumably single instance of poor judgment.

On the other hand, the *superego, too, not infrequently interferes with good judgment,* in neurotics and normals as well as in psychotics. There are those who feel, for instance, that John Foster Dulles's diplomacy was sometimes adversely affected by his evaluation of other nations according to his own moral standards.

Psychotic defects in judgment are most likely to be rooted in firm delusional systems, particularly of a paranoid nature; very intelligent patients are especially likely to use exquisite reality testing as a basis for acts which reflect poor judgment.

As just discussed, defects in judgment may occur with some degree of *independence* from reality testing, since *judgment involves a proper matching of perceived reality with memory material regarding social, physical, and other factors.* Apparently, the process of matching may be interfered with in minor or major ways by *fatigue, disruptive impulses, undue superego pressure,* or *failure either of superego functioning or of signal anxiety.* A businessman who is perfectly capable of judging contemporary reality may permit himself undue optimism and buy a trainload of lumber when a small truckload would do. Conversely, *depression may color judgment* so as to cause unduly pessimistic anticipations from relatively correctly perceived reality. *Anxiety may so radically affect* one's anticipation of consequences, despite correct perceptions of reality, as to lead to disastrous and even psychotic decisions.

Although defects in judgment may be relatively independent of reality testing, they are *usually* fused with defects in reality testing and are often combined with problems of impulse control and/or disturbances of defenses and other ego functions.

Treatment of poor judgment is largely treatment *of the factors underlying it,* that is, of elation, depression, anxiety, defective reality testing, poor impulse control, projection, and other disturbances of the defenses. Disruption of the stimulus barrier is sometimes serious enough to lead to poor judgment; for example, excessive stimulus overload may lead to anger and irritability which might cause one to make impetuous and ill-conceived decisions.

Patients who habitually use poor judgment need constant review of cause and effect. Sometimes prediction of poor judgment in specified circumstances will help to prevent it. Another important strategy for preventing acts based upon poor judgment is to request the patient to *agree to a delay* of the action—for instance, an ill-advised marriage or business deal. *Homicidal, suicidal, or delusional acts may lose their motivation* if the patient can be made to agree to postpone action. He will then retain his freedom of choice, except for a delay. Delay interferes with the pleasure of immediate impulse discharge, thus often obviating the need to act.

Frequently, an outstanding part of the treatment is to increase the patient's *"signal awareness"* or anticipation of mental sets or reality circumstances that are particularly likely to trigger poor judgment.

3) TREATMENT OF DISTURBANCES OF SENSE OF REALITY OF THE WORLD AND OF THE SELF

Disturbances in the sense of self are closely allied to disturbances of the sense of identity. The concepts of *identity crisis and loss of identity* are at present in wide use (from Erikson, Edith Jacobson, and Rosenfeld, to Laing and Sartre). Freeman, Cameron, and McGhie (1958) have placed a disturbance in the sense of self at the center of the schizophrenic disorder. In this they closely follow Federn's (1952) conception of an underlying disorder of self-boundaries, which he described primarily in terms of shifts of cathexis depleting healthy ego cathexis. Federn, and Freeman, Cameron, and McGhie put the emphasis upon the loss of what are the best called self-boundaries rather than ego-boundaries. Varying degrees of disturbance in the sense of self may, in fact, be caused by a variety of factors, and therefore treatment also varies a great deal (Bellak, 1964).

In some persons, the sense of self may never have developed well because of autistic or *symbiotic relations* with the maternal figure by virtue of poor, inconsistent introjects. A crucial factor in a poor sense of self lies in a conflict between two parts of the self, which results in an increase in the self-observing function of the ego. Withdrawal of libidinal energy from other outside objects may also play a role in a poor sense of self. On quite a different level, hysterical focusing on the distance when looking at near objects may also produce depersonalization and so may *hyperventilation,* with subsequent dizziness and changes in proprioception. Perceptual isolation, fatigue, and drugs (a paradoxical, anxiety-arousing effect of sedatives, for instance) may also cause hyperventilation. More than ordinary awareness of usually automatic functions, such as walking (onto a stage, for instance), may lead to what Simon (1967) calls the deautomatizing effect of consciousness.

Aside from interpretation of relevant dynamic aspects, depersonalization may be treated by *drugs* if it is caused by panic or if it is caused by *nuchal rigidity,* resulting from metabolic alkalosis caused by hyperventilation.

The more disturbed the patient, the more active the therapist must be in helping him *build* (or rebuild) *self-esteem and in helping him structure his life,* at least temporarily, so as to avoid self-esteem-destroying experiences. For example, the therapist should discourage the patient from taking on a larger task than he is likely to be able to manage. Specific self-concepts need analyzing; e.g., concretization of the self as something dirty, dangerous, and loathsome is frequent and needs great attention.

A few joint consultations with the patient and the important figures in his life may be very hlepful if there are specific disturbances of role perception, especially in relation to one or more of these significant people.

4) TREATMENT OF DISTURBANCES OF REGULATION AND
CONTROL OF DRIVE, AFFECT, AND IMPULSE

Poor regulation and control of drives are probably the most frequent cause for hospitalization of psychotics. Poor drive control causes more social disruption than most other ego function disturbances and is generally most easily perceived as a threat. Historically, unenlightened response to psychotic behavior primarily entailed an interference with freedom by chains and incarceration. When a person was said to be possessed by the devil, reference was almost always made to his loss of regulation and control of drives and impulses.

The more recent traditional forms of dealing with severe disturbances of drive regulation and control were restraining sheets, wet packs, various other hydrotherapeutic procedures, camisoles, and locked doors. These means of dealing with psychotic disturbances of control have been almost entirely replaced by chemical restraints, psychotropic drugs, and reform of hospital wards into therapeutic communities with patient government, nurses out of uniform, and open doors. Among the latest psychotropic drugs, lithium carbonate as a specific treatment of manic excitement is particularly relevant to the control of excessive drive.

Drugs play a crucial role not only generally in the treatment of psychotics but also in psychotherapy of non-psychotics and in the classical analysis of patients suffering extreme disturbances in drive regulation and control. In Ostow's (1962) hands, psychoanalysis of schizophrenics is made possible by a sort of "drug sandwich." Drugs of the phenothiazine variety are used to put a ceiling on the patient's drives, and stimulants, energizers, and antidepressants are used to establish a "bottom" (in terms of energy level). Via a method akin to titration, one can establish the most useful midpoint between excessive control and lack of control within which to carry on the analytic process.

The strictly psychotherapeutic treatment of a lack of drive regulation and control still has a large role to play. *Cathartic interpretation,* as practiced especially by John Rosen (1962), may be very useful for diminishing uncontrolled behavior or interfering with excessive control. Using interpretation to strengthen the superego, as well as to decrease the drives, is often an important strategy (Bellak, 1963). Typically, the superego of the very disturbed person is inconsistent—in part too severe and in part too lenient. The appropriate psychotherapeutic operations strive toward greater consistency by strengthening some parts and weakening others. In all grades of severity of acting-out, it is important to establish continuity for the patient in place of the discontinuity that exists through his use of denial, magical thinking, and other distortions. In addition, repeated prediction of the consequences of acting-out is a useful therapeutic strategy (Bellak, 1963). Excessive aggressive behavior may, of course, be a denial of fear of passivity. Recent studies suggest that if delusions of grandeur used as a means of inflating self-esteem are interfered with, violent actions, including homicide, are easily precipitated.

Very often a lack of regulation and control in an adult is caused by a lack of education, as well as by early overstimulation of aggressive and sexual drives. In such cases, the building of controls and the decrease of stimulation require a long, drawn-out therapeutic effort that strongly resembles education. Interpretation of apperceptive distortions (which incite excessive response from the patient) is a traditionally helpful intervention. If it is difficult to modify an inconsistent superego psychotherapeutically, it is even more difficult to bring about a progression of drive from pregenital to genital orientation, neutralization, and sublimation. Where strictly psychotherapeutic means do not suffice, active changes of the environment may be necessary: The butcher whose sadism is excessively stimulated in a butcher shop or the barber whose homosexuality is excessively aroused in a barber shop needs to be helped to change his occupation.

Above all, the patient needs to be helped to develop better signal awareness (i.e., awareness of a dangerous buildup of drive) and to develop the ability to respond appropriately before the drive becomes excessive.

Very general measures for tension reduction and drive reduction, such as vigorous exercise (especially in the presence of an excessive aggressive drive), may temporarily play a very useful role.

5) TREATMENT OF DISTURBANCES OF OBJECT RELATIONS

The nature of object relations is at the very heart of psychoanalytic theory. In a crisis situation, the poorer the object relations, the greater the danger for a serious disturbance, be it of psychotic nature or a suicidal threat.

It is, therefore, especially important to examine and strengthen object relations during a crisis. This is a time when the analyst or therapist may have to give up even the customary therapeutic neutrality and become more available and offer more direct support. It is important that this not be done in a way which by itself could be frightening to the patient or lead to a secondary need for revenge.

Negative transference needs to be carefully interpreted—the transference often being the most sensitive of all object relations while someone is in active analytic therapy.

Any factors involving the transference relationship can dramatically affect a patient, particularly a more disturbed patient. Routine events like vacations and illness can cause major emotional upheaval. In some patients, aggression or anxiety aroused by the therapist may lead to episodes of panic or depersonalization. In depressed patients, experience of rejection outside or in the therapeutic relationship may lead to depression and suicidal ideation. Jacobson (1971) vividly described the basic mechanisms involved in depression, as well as the parameters necessary in terms of treatment of the depressed, i.e., less therapeutic neutrality and more variation in the analyst's attitude in consonance with the patient's mood swings.

In treatment of borderline and schizophrenic patients, Boyer and Giovacchini (1967) and others have described the vicissitudes of object relations. The very term "object relations theory" underlines the protean nature of this sphere of functioning and its basic interactions with other functions.

Indeed, treatment of object relations is the core of treatment per se, and the discussion of the nature and problems of all the other ego functions involves object relations by implication.

6) TREATMENT OF DISTURBANCES OF THOUGHT PROCESSES

The close interconnection of thought processes with other ego functions has been emphasized by many. Cameron (1944), one of the earliest investigators, suggested that normal adult thinking is the result of repeated social communication and that disorganized schizophrenics have never developed adequate ability to empathize with the other with whom they wish to communicate. Disturbances of communication patterns originally identified within families (Singer and Wynne, 1966) and the double-bind concept of Bateson and Jackson (1956) continue to play important roles in the study of psychopathology. These conceptualizations all imply a close relationship between object relations and thought processes. It is evident that if a schizophrenic thought disorder is caused by the failure of persons to develop, among other things, syllogistic thinking because of poor object relations or disturbed communications patterns with other people, particularly parents, with whom they grew up, the establishment of thought processes via good object relations in individual therapy, group therapy, or rehabilitation workshop plays a major role in correcting the disorder.

Investigators from diverse backgrounds all tend to agree that *anxiety* and other emotions may interfere with thought processes and lead to a regression, developmentally speaking, from secondary-process to primary-process thinking. As a behaviorist, Mednick (1958) sees thought disorder in terms of *conditioned avoidance;* i.e., when a thought makes one anxious, it is avoided by, for example, overgeneralization—the opposite of "calling a spade a spade," but rather beating around the bush, resulting in tangentiality and circumstantiality or in the extreme, loose associations.

Psychoanalysts, on the other hand, see disturbances in thought processes as a defense. On the basis of these hypotheses, it is obvious that treatment of thought disorder must often address itself to anxiety and other disturbing affects. One approach may be the use of drugs, another may employ psychotherapy, or a combination of the two. A study by Bellak and Chassan (1964) suggested that Librium and psychotherapy are able to reduce primary-process thinking; the phenothiazines are well known to be especially able to ameliorate a thought disorder in the severely disturbed. Such improvement can be attained relatively easily if good secondary-process thinking has been attained by the patient in the past. Constant review of external and internal events for the patient may increase synthetic functioning and show him logical relationships between cause and effect.

Evidence of the Valium effect and clinical evidence from psychotherapy suggest that any therapeutic intervention—drug or psychotherapy—which reduces anxiety improves all ego functions and, specifically, thought processes.

If one becomes aware of actual gaps in the patient's thinking, it is important to illustrate them to him repeatedly. For example, sometimes thought processes are discontinuous because the patient is simply too narcissistic to engage in the "role playing" that Cameron (1944) considers essential to good thought processes, i.e., taking the role of someone who communicates his thoughts and feelings while keeping in mind the particular person with whom he is conversing. In other words, Cameron saw at the root of the problem that the patient is too self-involved to pay attention to whether the thoughts expressed are intelligible to the listener. If the patient reveals overinclusive thinking, which so many consider the most frequent and basic disorder in schizophrenic thinking, again it is important to illustrate this to him and to interpret the reasons for his doing it.

7) TREATMENT OF DISTURBANCES OF ADAPTIVE REGRESSION IN THE SERVICE OF THE EGO (ARISE)

Unlike work with other ego functions, a relative reduction of creativity (Adaptive Regression In the Service of the Ego—ARISE) in the therapy of psychotics may play a desirable and important part in bringing about a strengthening of defenses against the emergence of primary-process material. Therefore, plans for facilitating regression in some patients should be very carefully weighed, since the price in terms of disorganization, panic, or even dangerous acting-out may be too high. Sometimes, as a relatively desperate measure, a decrease of ARISE may be a therapeutic goal precisely in the attempt to stem an influx of overwhelming psychotic thought. If nothing else helps, some therapists have suggested not only avoiding interference with, but also actively encouraging fads, "obsessive" occupations, or interest in religious ritual, as forms of defense at the cost of ARISE. Parenthetically, it may be remarked that rather healthy siblings of psychotics often suffer from constriction and loss of ARISE because they are afraid "to be crazy" like their brother or sister—in essence, a phobic defense.

Dynamic psychotherapy may be affected by a disturbance of ARISE because a lack of tolerance of ambiguity is involved. Syllogisms, which are the basis for all dynamic interpretations, are impossible for the patient to grasp. In the extreme, concrete thinking is present. Patients with disturbances of ARISE, even if not psychotic, cannot possibly tell a story about a T.A.T. card other than to offer the most straightforward description. In such patients it is the first phase of the oscillating process that is disturbed. No decrease in perceptual acuity is permitted. In the workaday world there are many borderline psychotics who function by virtue of doing the same thing in the same way every day of their lives, and those in contact with them soon discover the futility of any attempt to get them to react adaptively to a change in circumstances.

A psychotherapeutic attempt to change this rigidity can sometimes be predicated on illustrating to them that other people see things differently, or see different things in the Rorshach and other tests, or have many varied stories to tell for the T.A.T. pictures. Long ago Bellak suggested that barbiturates (sometimes mixed with stimulants) may help produce the first phase of ARISE in the psychotherapeutic session and provide an avenue for further work (Bellak, 1949). Interpretation of extremely rigid defenses may be helpful. In patients given to very concrete thinking, decreasing the equation of a thought with an act will also decrease anxiety and produce more adaptive ability.

Extreme disturbance of the first phase of the oscillating process necessary for ARISE is more often seen in people best diagnosed as psychotic characters than in obsessive characters.

An extreme ability to regress in the first phase, combined with insufficient ability to return to adaptive structural functioning in the second phase, characterizes psychotics in their artistic productions as well as in their other activities. Such people often appear to be gifted not only artistically but in many other ways. Structurally or educationally, however, they do not have enough adaptive potential for their efforts to lead to any fruition. Psychotherapy to strengthen reality testing and drive control is necessary. There are probably exceptional people in whom a disturbance in the second phase of ARISE coexists with congenital ability or acquired structural and adaptive characteristics of such strength that, although they are psychotic for all other purposes, their productions are still artistic in the sense of communicating powerfully to others (rather than having only private meaning). In such instances, strengthening of the adaptive functions by psychotherapy, training (for instance, learning the craft aspects of their art), and drugs is indicated.

8) TREATMENT OF DISTURBANCES OF DEFENSIVE FUNCTIONING

The treatment of the disturbance of the defensive functions preeminently involves, of course, insight psychotherapy shedding light on the primary impulses, the apperceptive distortions, and the inappropriate defenses. In part, treatment can parallel the therapeutic interventions for loss of drive control—for example, manipulation of the environment to decrease stimuli, changes in vocation, living place, and habits. Drugs are useful. The therapist must assess dynamics quickly and, if the patient is psychotic, even insist upon drastic changes rather than staying aloof from decisions that involve reality.

In taking an ego function approach to therapy, the *importance of general dynamic understanding must be stressed.* This includes the likelihood that the decreased effectiveness of ego functions is the result of a defensive attempt to avoid anxiety. Thus, in psychotherapy, attempts to improve the adaptiveness of a given ego function include interpreting to the patient the defensive aspect of his symptoms and interpreting the nature of the material being defended against.

Interference with ego functions as a result of defensive reactions must be distinguished from secondary interference resulting from regression of another ego function. For example, poor memory will secondarily affect problem-solving and other ego functions.

The development of psychoanalytic practice has resulted in a degree of condescension toward the use of intellectualization as a therapeutic device, if not outright disapproval of it. The emphasis upon the cathartic experience, with insight accompanied by affective changes, undoubtedly is responsible for intellectualization being relegated to a position of disrepute. Nonetheless, as a practical matter, if the development of a defense previously only slightly used by the patient results in a decrease in use of a more pathological defense, then a psychotherapeutic change has been brought about. The effect of intellectualization, therefore, has a proper place in the practice of psychotherapy. Knowledge where there has been misinformation, reality where there has been fantasy, often go a long way toward relieving the anxiety patients experience as a result of lack of information. Every psychotherapist has had the experience of immediate amelioration of anxiety when a patient has learned that his symptoms are, for example, not unique, but are rather widely experienced. Combatting distortions attendant to masturbation are perhaps a prime example. In cases where anger is generated in a relationship, we have effectively stated that many people respond with anger to situations in which they actually experience fear. This idea has been helpful in enabling the patient to contain the reaction based on rage, while intellectually he searches for those aspects of the relationship which may be generating anxiety. The effect of intellectualization is often to cut through denial, and thus assist in making that which is preconscious conscious, in turn permitting eventually a more insightful type of learning.

Much of the pain of anxiety and other symptoms derives from the feeling of helplessness vis-à-vis the symptoms. The patient feels attacked by an unseen antagonist or force. Intellectual presentation of the cause of depression, or of displacement and somatization in hysteria, for example, can impart optimism and motivation to cooperate in psychotherapy.

Intellectualization is most useful in giving the patient a new way of looking at his behavior. It provides a start on a new approach to to his problems, an approach that might never occur to him spontaneously.

9) TREATMENT OF DISTURBANCES OF STIMULUS BARRIER

The stimulus barrier has not usually been treated as an ego function. The argument against doing so has been based on the idea that the stimulus barrier is a congenital given, rather than a result of development or experience.

It is questionable whether stimulus barrier is more of a congenital factor than some other autonomous ego functions. Certainly, the nature of the stimulus barrier may also be the result of early infantile, and even later, experiences. Excessive stimulation of infants and cramped, noisy quarters probably raise both the stimulus barrier and the arousal level; such people may be in a higher state of arousal and need more stimulation (stimulus hunger) (Bellak & Berneman, 1971), but at the same time have a higher barrier against input.

It is conceivable that a low stimulus barrier may coexist with a disturbed electroencephalogram in some individuals. A study of the electrical functioning of the brain may be useful.

Some physiological states, such as premenstrual water retention and changes in the electrolyte balance, lower the stimulus barrier and are probably frequently responsible for many marital conflicts. Conversely, dehydrating drugs frequently upset the electrolyte balance, which may in turn seriously affect the normal stimulus barrier.

Certain social conditions, such as the sharing of one room day and night by a large number of impoverished people, may result in such tremendous aggressive, sexual, and other overstimulation as to cause a lack of, or loss of, control and certainly interfere with optimal development. Only socioeconomic changes are likely to solve those problems.

Therapeutically, one may have to take advantage of whatever environmental changes are possible. Changes in living conditions are sometimes possible. Changes in vocation or daily routine designed to avoid a stimulus "overload" may be essential for the prevention of further ego disorganization.

Tranquilizers may in part have their effect by increasing the stimulus barrier. The effect of lithium on manic states has been ascribed by some to its slowing down the processing of information. Lithium does not seem to have that effect on schizophrenics; however, phenothiazines may well play a role in increasing the stimulus barrier in schizophrenics. Overideational states, as well as catatonic excitement, might well be the result of overload of inner stimuli. There is some clinical evidence that catatonic stupor is, among other things, an attempt to decrease stimulus input (as well as to control affect).

10) TREATMENT OF DISTURBANCES OF AUTONOMOUS FUNCTIONING

The need for relative intactness of autonomous functions for the work of classical psychoanalysis has been pointed out by Loewenstein (1966, 1967, 1972); his broad definition of autonomous functions includes reality testing, anticipation, and self-observation.

In psychotics, the primary autonomous functions, such as memory, intention, movement, and language, may be severely afflicted. Nevertheless, even within impaired areas some aspects of secondary autonomy may remain remarkably intact. A patient who stood around in a frozen catatonic stance could play rapid and brilliant ping-pong once he was positioned to receive the ball at the end of the table. A kind of automatized function seemed to take over. As soon as the ball dropped from the table, by his or his opponent's doing, he froze back into a catatonic stance. Continued attempts to play ping-pong with him led to an increasing continuity of movement within the table-tennis setting and later to an abandonment of catatonic rigidity in other situations.

Special skills other than motor ones often resist psychotic impairment. Many a person with severe defects in reality testing, judgment, and control of impulses remains a skilled worker and retains special information—even several foreign languages—or professional competence. In such cases the still-intact functions are most important, as they may be used in an attempt to improve the defective functions.

11) TREATMENT OF DISTURBANCES OF SYNTHETIC-INTEGRATIVE FUNCTIONING

The treatment of disturbed synthetic function may proceed by strengthening other ego functions and by dealing with drive disturbances impairing the synthetic function. Drugs may also be useful. It may be necessary to advise the patient to decrease his burdens, at least temporarily. In such a case the decrease in demands is analogous to the splinting of a broken limb and permits the synthetic function to improve again almost spontaneously. In patients who have particular difficulty in synthesizing affect and thought, it is essential to establish continuity where they experience discontinuity.

It is very likely that perceptual motor disturbances, to which increasing attention is being paid in connection with dyslexia and other learning difficulties, are related to some problems of synthetic functioning in the young and that educational help is necessary. In some such children, because of a primary lack of synthesis or perhaps a secondary continued frustration over their inability to perform routine motor and perceptual tasks, emotional explosiveness may also be part of a failure of the synthetic function.

Inconsistent upbringing is certainly likely to impede the maturation of synthetic functioning, and prevention of disturbances is ultimately the treatment of choice.

12) TREATMENT OF DISTURBANCES OF MASTERY-COMPETENCE

A feeling of impotence toward the forces of life, of an inability to master or alter them, seems characteristic of man, particularly in the post-World War II period and the atomic age. Existentialism (philosophical and literary) concerns itself primarily with man's relation to powerful forces. Camus' literary characters are helpless, confused, and at the mercy of both their drives and fate. Laing (1960), who is probably the most widely known latter-day exponent of the existential viewpoint in psychiatry, deals specifically with the schizophrenic living in today's world.

An improvement of object relations or impulse control, of reality testing or judgment, is bound to have an indirect effect upon mastery and competence. Self-esteem is, of course, related to the sense of competence. Many outstanding psychotic delusions and hallucinations are the direct result of disturbances in self-esteem, in objective competence, and in the subjective feeling of competence. Classically, delusions of grandeur—frequently encountered in schizophrenic patients with paranoid and/or manic disturbances—both defend against, and are intricately interwoven with, a deep feeling of impotence. A schizophrenic, especially one with manic tendencies, may well imagine himself to be an exalted personage. This easily leads to paranoid delusions—for example, that because he is so important, not only are many people interested in him but many are also inimical to him and eager to put him out of the way. At the heart of these grandiose feelings and the paranoid ones are feelings of smallness and passivity. One could well say that the psychotic makes himself so big because he feels so small; he feels so powerful and conceives of such powerful enemies because he feels so weak and helpless when it comes to affecting himself and his world.

Central to the treatment of disturbances of mastery and competence, therefore, is the treatment of low self-esteem. Such therapy may involve interpreting the pathological means of inflating or otherwise regulating self-esteem and dealing with whatever precipitated the particular instance of lowered self-esteem. For example, a patient's delusion of being extremely wealthy may have started with a business failure of objectively rather small proportions but of great importance to him in terms of his actual and subjective sense of mastery-competence. On the other hand, people with a high degree of mastery and competence as part of their life history tend to have a good prognosis in psychotherapy almost independent of the degree of their psychopathology.

REFERENCES

BATESON, G., JACKSON, D. et al. Toward a theory of schizophrenia. *Behavioral Science*, 1, 251-264, 1956.

BELLAK, L. The use of oral barbiturates in psychotherapy. *American Journal of Psychiatry*, 105:849-850, 1949.

BELLAK, L. Acting Out: Some conceptual and therapeutic considerations. *American Journal of Psychotherapy*, 17:375-389, 1963.

BELLAK, L. Depersonalization as a variant of self-awareness. In A. Abrams (Ed.), *Unfinished Tasks in the Behavioral Sciences*. Baltimore: Williams and Wilkins, 1964.

BELLAK, L. & BERNEMAN, N. A systematic view of depression. *American Journal of Psychotherapy*, 25 (3):385-393, 1971.

BELLAK, L. & CHASSAN, J. B. An approach to the evaluation of drug effect during psychotherapy: A double-blind study of a single case. *Journal of Nervous and Mental Disease*, 139:20-30, 1964.

BELLAK, L. & MEYERS, B. Ego function assessment and analyzability. *International Journal of Psycho-Analysis*, Vol. 2, Part 4, 413-427, 1975.

BOYER, L. & GIOVACCHINI, P. *Psychoanalytic Treatment of Characterological and Schizophrenic Disorders*. New York: Science House, 1967.

CAMERON, N. Experimental analysis of schizophrenic thinking (1944). In J. Kasanin (Ed.), *Language and Thought in Schizophrenia*. New York: Norton, 1964, pp. 50-64.

FEDERN, P. Some variations in ego feeling (1926). In E. Weiss (Ed.), *Ego Psychology and the Psychoses*. New York: Basic Books, 1952.

FREEMAN, T., CAMERON, J., & McGHIE, A. *Chronic Schizophrenia*. New York: International Universities Press, 1958.

JACOBSON, E. *Depression: Comparative Studies of Normal, Neurotic and Psychotic Conditions*. New York: International Universities Press, 1971.

LAING, R. *The Divided Self*. Chicago: Quadrangle, 1960.

LOEWENSTEIN, R. On the theory of the superego: A discussion. In R. Loewenstein, L. Newman, M. Schur & A. Solnit (Eds.), *Psychoanalysis: A General Psychology*. New York: International Universities Press, 1966.

LOEWENSTEIN, R. Defensive organization and autonomous ego functions. *Journal of the American Psychoanalytic Association*, 15, 795-809, 1967.

LOEWENSTEIN, R. Ego autonomy and psychoanalytic technique. *Psychoanalytic Quarterly*, 41, 1972.

MEDNICK, S. A learning theory approach to research in schizophrenia (1958). In: A. Buss & E. Buss (Eds.), *Theories of Schizophrenia*. New York: Atherton Press, 1969.

OSTOW, M. *Drugs in Psychoanalysis and Psychotherapy*. New York: Basic Books, 1962.

ROSEN, J. *Direct Analysis*. New York: Grune & Stratton, 1953.

ROSEN, J. *Direct Psychoanalytic Psychiatry*. New York: Grune & Stratton, 1962.

SIMON, J. The paradoxical effect of effort. *British Journal of Medical Psychology*, 40, 1967, 375.

SINGER, M. & WYNNE, L. Principles for scoring communication defects and deviances in parents of schizophrenics: Rorschach and T.A.T. scoring manuals. *Psychiatry*, 29, 1966, 260.

6. Utilizing External Facilities

Working with the very disturbed patient, it is important to be aware of the *resources* in the community. Naturally, one has to make oneself more available to the more impaired patients than to the less disturbed ones. If one works with such patient populations, the first line of support must be the close relationship with one or more colleagues who can be called upon if the primary therapist or analyst is not available. These must be colleagues who are acquainted with and capable of dealing with emergency situations ad hoc. If there is particular reason to expect a flare-up in a patient, especially while one is on a vacation, it is best if, with the patient's permission, a colleague is informed of his current condition and the nature of his current and most pressing problems. If, for some reason, the closely affiliated colleague is not available, it is important that one point out to the patient the existence of other resources. For example, most communities have hotlines for crisis intervention and suicide prevention 24 hours around the clock. Also, there are social agencies which may make themselves available for specific needs. Above all, however, for a very disturbed person, it is important to be able to enlist family support if and when necessary.

In the case of the severely neurotic, the borderline, and the psychotic patient, it is also important that one is aware of *the human resources in the patient's life* in case of an emergency or generally difficult situations. *It is important to have the addresses and phone numbers of one or more close relatives and/or friends, especially if there is no spouse, in the event the patient should become suicidal or otherwise severely disturbed.* Under such circumstances, it should be possible to call on such contacts to remain in physical proximity to the patient and it must be possible for us to share with some person or persons closely related to the patient our concern about him. Of course, all these arrangements should be carried out with the patient's permission and knowledge.

Similarly, it is important to know who the patient's *family doctor* or internist is, again with the patient's permission. It is useful to let the internist know that the patient is in treatment with us and possibly on an active drug: If the patient overdoses, the family doctor or internist will be in a much better position to deal with medical emergencies if he has prior knowledge.

Group psychotherapy may be considered as an adjunct to psychotherapeutic learning either as a follow-up measure or running concomitantly with individual treatment. The unlearning and relearning acquired in individual therapy may need to be supplemented by often repeated experiences of a certain kind. Group therapy involves learning the consequences of maladaptive behavior patterns and offers support and reinforcement for more adaptive healthier behavior. This may help build impulse control and achieve other restructurings unattainable by verbal abstractions in the very best of individual therapy.

DRUGS AS ADJUNCTS TO PSYCHOTHERAPY

The Clinical Rationale

The clinical rationale, as opposed to the etiological or theoretical, is the most frequent one for combining pharmacotherapy and psychotherapy. In the broadest sense, one could say that often the psychotropic drugs play the same role for the therapist as anesthesia plays for the surgeon: They provide the enabling conditions for performing the psychotherapeutic operations. Drugs are often necessary because psychotherapy might not be possible without them, at least not on an ambulatory basis and not outside the hospital.

This rationale holds true for the extremely panicky neurotic, the depressed person, and the schizophrenic patient. The panicky patient can hold a job and function in the home with the help of the so-called minor tranquilizers, the anxiolytic drugs such as diazepam, meprobamate or diazepoxide. The drug may also enable him to talk about subject matter which he might otherwise avoid because of "approach anxiety."

The depressed patient who was relatively immobile and inarticulate prior to drug treatment can be helped with antidepressants—the tricyclics, monoamine oxydase inhibitors or others—to discuss his feelings and symptoms. Except for the use of phenothiazines and related substances, many schizophrenic patients might not be able to remain outside an institution or, if they could, might be so disturbed by hallucinations or delusions that communication would be difficult, if not impossible, to establish. Though the psychotropic drugs do not offer a cure per se, they often promote the crucial emotional and cognitive climate which enables the dynamic psychotherapy to take place that would otherwise be at best difficult, and occasionally impossible.

Two case histories illustrate the combined use of psychotherapy and pharmacotherapy.

A college student was admitted to the clinic for brief therapy because of anxiety attacks before and during certain classes. It was close to examination time, and his inability to attend these classes put him in danger of losing credit for the whole school year.

The dynamics of the situation became clear in the first session and had to do with voyeuristic and exhibitionistic wishes. In his circumstances even five weeks of psychotherapy was too long to wait for remediation. He therefore was given 25 mg. of diazepoxide to be taken one-and-a-half hours before each class. He was told to take the drug this early in the hope that it would prevent the development of anticipatory anxiety which in turn would be likely to escalate.

Meanwhile, the phobia could be treated psychotherapeutically and etiologically—something which the drug alone could not do. Since the therapeutic timetable was affected by the reality of examinations, somewhat more than the usual five sessions were needed to

deal with the phobia. After the examinations were passed successfully, a few additional sessions were used, sometimes several months
apart, when anxiety-producing situations arose again. At times diazepoxide was used, again with the explanation to the patient that
each instance of anxiety he mastered would constitute a valuable
form of deconditioning, in addition to the gains made by insight.
Two years later in a phone call he informed the therapist that he
had successfully graduated from college and accepted his first job.

Another case, while not strictly an example of the use of pharmacotherapy in combination with psychotherapy, is an excellent illustration of the use of drugs to provide enabling conditions to carry
on any kind of psychotherapy.

A young man, already in therapy with someone else for a severe
compulsion neurosis, was seen in consultation. It quickly became
apparent that an extensive toilet ritual—lasting a minimum of one
hour—caused him either to be at least a half-hour late for his regular
psychotherapy appointment or to miss it altogether.

The recommendation was to take 50 mg. chlorpromazine with 50
mg. imipramine HS. The considerations were dynamic. We know
that aggression plays a marked role in compulsive urges. We know
also, from experiments with artificially aroused primates, that chlorpromazine controls aggression; therefore chlorpromazine was per-
scribed. The imipramine, on the other hand, was necessary to
counteract the soporific, energy-sapping effect of the chlorpromazine
and also to counteract the depressive features that coexisted with the
compulsion neurosis.

In this case the immediate reason for the pharmacotherapy was
strictly clinical—one can't treat a patient who isn't there—although
the conceptualization of the case relied on psychoanalytic theory.

Of course, tardiness is also a problem for many depressed patients
who may not be able to get out of bed and/or suffer from psycho-
motor retardation. As part of this syndrome, such patients are often
unable to verbalize optimally. The use of antidepressants facilitates
utilization of psychotherapy. The patient gets to his appointment and
can communicate, so that even brief psychotherapy often may be
promptly effective. Because imipramine and amitriptyline may take

more than a week to become effective, methylphenidate is sometimes combined with imipramine or amitriptyline for its immediate antidepressant effect. The methylphenidate can be stopped as soon as the imipramine or amitriptyline becomes effective. To date no one treated by us has shown any tendency toward addiction or habituation to methylphenidate. It must be noted that these patients were not only carefully selected, but also closely supervised. In many drug clinics the patient is seen for a few minutes, at best, before being handed a prescription. In psychotherapy the patient is carefully evaluated prior to prescribing a drug or drugs. The subsequent therapeutic interviews provide the opportunity to monitor the patient's reactions to the drugs. The patient is further offered the support of the psychotherapeutic relationship, in addition to the beneficial effects of pharmacotherapy. People coming from a culture promoting drug abuse are excluded from medication by methylphenidate. Unless selectivity, caution, and supervision are used, it is better to avoid methylphenidate.

Some practitioners prefer MAO inhibitors for acute depressions because they take effect more quickly. The MAO inhibitors are generally less in favor because several foods,, some wines, cheeses, pickled herring, etc. tend to produce hypertensive reactions.

In the treatment of affective disorders, lithium carbonate plays a special role, particularly in the care of hypomanics and manics. Since the therapeutic dose is close to the toxic dose, careful monitoring of lithium serum levels is necessary. The combination of lithium therapy and psychotherapy facilitates both understanding the precipitating events and attempts to work through the dynamics, thus decreasing the chances of a recurrence of similar circumstances and similar manic reactions, both on a biochemical and psychodynamic basis.

Other Considerations

Drugs also may be used in psychotherapy on the basis of structural as well as psychodynamic and metapsychological rationales. The assessment of ego functions may be a basis for the metapsychological rationale. For example, if regulation and control of drives are poor, chlorpromazine may be indicated until something presumably can be done psychotherapeutically about impulsive acting-out. Psychotherapy of an acutely exacerbated chronic psychosis may be greatly facilitated by a phenothiazine which improves the nature of the thought processes enough so that the patient can be engaged in psychotherapy. This combination is obviously more helpful than either pharmacotherapy or psychotherapy alone. Ego-function assessment (see Chapter 3) is useful as a guide when considering which combination of drugs to use during psychotherapy.

Ostow's (1962) suggestion for the use of a mixture of tranquilizers and stimulants is basically related to an economic point of view. He hypothesizes that stimulants increase the available ego-libido while tranquilizers reduce it. On that basis he suggests a process similar to chemical titration, a process in which attempts are made by trial-and-error to find the optimal combination of the two drugs. Whether or not the theory underlying his suggestion is valid, clinically the judicious mixture of these two classes of drugs is often successful, thus providing what may be termed a therapeutic validation.

An important indicator for the use of drugs combined with therapy may exist when a patient has so much secondary gain from his symptoms that he is unwilling to give them up. This may happen with people who have suffered from a long, chronic illness or with people on welfare, who have derived some pleasure in the passivity afforded them under the circumstances. A stimulant drug, given for just a few days, will frequently enable them to get past their resistance to a point where they can again derive more pleasure from activity than passivity, gain some realistic advantages and significantly increase their sense of self-esteem.

Dynamically, it would be desirable to have a drug which could weaken superego forces. While the superego may be dissolved in alcohol, this approach is neither reliable nor practical.

A psychobiological basis for using drugs in psychotherapy is inherent in the catecholamine hypothesis and in other theories conceptualizing the etiology and pathogenesis of the psychoses in biochemical terms. There is little doubt that a continuous interaction exists between experience and a broad spectrum of biochemical processes, including endocrine secretions. Diurnal variation of secretions almost certainly has an effect on cognition as well as mood; eventually drugs and psychotherapy related to these biochemical changes will likely become especially efficacious.

Similarly, neurophysiological factors in disturbances such as minimal brain dysfunction need special mediation to optimize the ability to communicate in psychotherapy, to control impulses, to enhance concept formation, and to decrease anxiety.

Drugs may also be used for their placebo effect, either because of oral gratification or the production of natural substances such as endorphins. Sometimes even a soft drink, coffee, weak alcoholic beverage, fruit, or cookies may play this role in psychotherapy. Recommending their use with some patients helps to establish a therapeutic alliance, a rapport, a friendly atmosphere. The patient's response to these suggestions or to an inactive drug will test whether a placebo effect is being obtained. If it is, the therapist may elect to continue this procedure or to use an active drug to combine the placebo response and the physiological effect of the chemical agent.

Naturally, the use of drugs creates as well as solves some problems. As in all cases, advantages have to weighed against disadvantages and risks. It must be kept in mind that, in a very simple way, the mere act of administering drugs introduces parameters in the therapeutic relationship and the transference relationship. Unconsciously, giving drugs may constitute a feeding or a poisoning to the patient. It may mean a vote of no confidence. It may induce a fear of loss of control. Giving too much of an anxiolytic or antidepressant drug may seriously decrease the patient's motivation for dynamic work and insight, and prevent the basic restructuring that only psychotherapy can provide.

It is, therefore, important for the patient to understand that in most instances the drugs, as part of the therapeutic alliance, are merely auxiliary measures and not curative by themselves. It is also important to remember that at times the best drugs have a variety of disturbing side-effects. The fear of loss of control may produce paradoxical anxiety on a strictly psychological basis. On a somatic basis, many of the drugs produce cognitive changes and at times affect the muscles so as to impair proprioception; in such cases patients complain about feelings of depersonalization and derealization, of feeling "spaced out." It is well-known that many of the major tranquilizers have a long list of side-effects. The most frequent and innocuous of these are dryness of the mouth, some blurring of vision, and some soporific effect. A more serious potential effect on the nervous system are Parkinsonian-like side-effects associated with phenothiazines. Some of the antidepressants can produce paranoid ideation or precipitate manic attacks. The therapist using drugs should thoroughly familiarize himself with their various mechanisms of actions and various effects and instruct the patient carefully in their use.

Despite their possibly undesirable aspects, psychotropic drugs are important, sometimes by themselves, and often as adjuncts in the hands of the skilled psychotherapist.

THE BRIEF HOSPITALIZATION

Situations arise in the emergency treatment of both suicidal or borderline psychotic patients where outpatient treatment cannot proceed safely. A period of hospitalization in a general hospital provides both the required protection of the patient and the conditions of safety and scrutiny which permit the psychotherapist to make vigorous in-depth interpretations, producing both catharsis and ego-mending as a result. Acute delusional states of recent precipitation may also be treatable under such circumstances.

Every clinician and facility treating very ill patients should have easy access to a hospital for admitting a patient who may suddenly need hospitalization. It is equally desirable (though more difficult to arrange especially with university-affiliated hospitals) that the clinician be permitted to continue emergency therapy with the patient during his hospitalization; the patient is often particularly amenable to active treatment in this protected environment.

Equally important is the ability to keep the hospitalization short and to have the patient promptly discharged. Therapeutically speaking, many patients in emergency therapy may decompensate quickly but also reconstitute promptly. Prolonged hospitalization often produces unnecessary and undesirable regression.

Though the above recommendations, i.e., ease of admission, continuing therapy in the hospital by the primary and original therapist, and ease of discharge, are simple and basic, they often are difficult to arrange. Institutional red tape, professional rivalries, insurance coverage, and other problems often interfere with this optimal arrangement.

In the outpatient clinics of hospitals providing emergency psychotherapy, an even simpler device is desirable: namely the arrangement of two or three beds in a room adjoining the clinic where some patients can be kept 12 to 24 hours, to help them bridge a specific crisis. Because of the scarcity of space in most hospitals and clinics, even this modest variation of emergency psychotherapy often runs into difficulties.

ENABLING CONDITIONS AND CONTRAINDICATIONS

For all patients, and especially for the more disturbed patient, the therapist should clearly establish existing resources in the patient's life and community which he can utilize should an emergency arise. If, for example, there is no one reliable, responsible, and reasonably stable in the patient's life and the patient is a borderline or psychotic individual, taking this patient into ambulatory treatment may be contraindicated. In such a case it is very likely that situations will arise, including severe emergencies, which will be too anxiety-producing for both the patient and the therapist to permit the necessary therapeutic work to be done. Similarly, community resources, hospitals, social services, auxiliary therapists, etc. should be available and readily accessible to the clinician. Reasonable geographic and economic stability should also be considered as factors enabling productive therapy and avoiding prohibitive transference and countertransference problems. Some therapists feel that patient-therapist "matching" should be weighed into the balance.

REFERENCE

Ostow, M. *Drugs in Psychoanalysis and Psychotherapy.* New York: Basic Books, 1962.

7. Special Problems in Treating Ambulatory Psychotics: Ten Enabling Conditions

The psychotherapy of acutely disturbed psychotics can be one of the most rewarding of therapeutic experiences. It is frequently possible to effect a dramatic loss of symptoms and general improvement of the acute manifestations of the disorder rather promptly. It often enough holds true that after the acute phase has been successfully dealt with, there remain the characterological features which are of complex nature and that often require prolonged and patient treatment. The present discussion, however, addresses itself only to the circumstances necessary for the treatment of the acute phase of a schizophrenic episode.

Certainly, the first question that must arise in the treatment of an acutely disturbed psychotic on an ambulatory basis, in the private office, social agency, or a clinic, must be whether a patient is suitable for this type of treatment.

Therefore, I want to address myself to the necessary conditions, the conditions that enable one to perform ambulatory psychotherapy

Reprinted from *Specialized Techniques in Individual Psychotherapy*, edited by Toksoz Karasu and Leopold Bellak, Brunner/Mazel, Inc., New York, 1980, by permission of the co-editor and publisher.

with psychotics. If the enabling conditions outlined cannot be met, ambulatory psychotherapy may not be advisable, and an alternate mode of treatment may be indicated.

1) *A Reasonably Cooperative, Non-assaultive Patient*

One of the most obvious enabling conditions is that one has to have a *reasonably cooperative, non-assaultive patient.* By reasonably cooperative, I mean that he at least comes to the session or is willing to be brought by a third party. However, it may be possible to start psychotherapy with a patient who is unwilling to come to therapy. Sometimes it is necessary to visit the patient in his own home, at least to initiate therapy. When this is not possible or feasible, an effective means of getting an unwilling patient to the office is to instruct a family member to ask the patient to accompany him to see the psychotherapist for his—the relative's—own sake. It is usually true enough that the relative is deeply concerned and upset, and is being sincere when he tells the patient that he wants some help for dealing with some of his own problems. Often the patient is then willing to come along as a mute companion. The initial exchanges are all between the therapist and the patient's relative. It must be part of the therapist's skill to eventually engage the patient until he or she slowly becomes the main interactor and ultimately the sole one.

One other possibility of engaging a patient in treatment, if the above procedure is ineffectual, is to engage in *mediate interpretations.* If a patient refuses to come by himself or even with a companion, as described above, it may be possible to learn enough about the psychodynamics of the patient from the relative to suggest statements or interpretations which the relative can then relay back to the patient. If, in turn, the relative reports back to the therapist, he can be used to mediate the therapy in such a way that the patient might be affected beneficially enough to a point where he is willing to come for treatment with the relative as companion. Then the therapist can proceed as above.

The fact that many schizophrenics may start out mute or barely communicative is no contraindication to therapy. Even potential assaultiveness need not be a contraindication, provided one sets up certain conditions which I will discuss later, with regard to certain precautions and the possible concomitant use of drugs. Of course, I include patients in ambulatory psychotherapy who are often actively deluded and hallucinated. Most of us are aware of the fact that in many patients extensive delusions and hallucinations need not necessarily interfere in seemingly normal social behavior. There is many a patient who thinks he is Jesus Christ or believes he can understand what the birds are saying, but nevertheless may continue to hold a skilled job and arrive punctually for each of his appointments. Although some patients may not be well enough to come on their own by car or bus, they may still profit from ambulatory psychotherapy, if someone brings them to the therapist's office.

The premise is that, whenever possible, it is better to avoid hospitalization, provided the patient is not actively homicidal or suicidal or so disturbed as to do harm inadvertently. The fact is that very little competent psychotherapy is offered in any hospital. In university-affiliated institutions, residents are usually the ones directly treating the patient, even though under supervision. Though they may be competent, the fact is they are still at an early stage of their training. In private institutions, there are usually not enough psychotherapists available, or else the therapists available are of questionable competence. The cost of hospitalization often approaches $100,-000 a year. In addition, regression and secondary gain from being cared for ("nursed") produce other problems. Very frequently, the patient's reentry into the community, if it is not extremely skillfully handled, starts a new flare-up.

2) One Stable Relationship in the Patient's Life

Less obvious and less generally considered is the almost absolute need for at least *one stable relationship in the patient's life situation* —at least one person, such as parent, spouse, child, close friend— anybody whom one might turn to if the circumstances should warrant it. The therapist must be able to talk to somebody who is willing to keep an eye on the patient at home, because of concerns about suicide, or other potentially harmful situations; someone who can take a helpful role if the patient should require hospitalization, or can otherwise serve as a constructive influence in the patient's life. Without at least a single stable person close to the patient, I have found through bitter experience that one may be left with almost impossible situations, more responsibility than one can reasonably handle, and with less safety than is essential for the treatment situation.

3) A Close Relationship with a Nearby Hospital

The third enabling condition for anybody who wants to treat rather acutely disturbed psychotics is that one have a *close relationship with a nearby hospital,* including a general hospital willing to take psychiatric patients. It is essential in treating acute psychotics that one be willing to take reasonable risks. Those reasonable risks include the possibility that some patients will become more disturbed in the course of treatment, either for adventitious reasons or for reasons intrinsic to the treatment. The therapist can engage in psychotherapy with acutely disturbed people only if he feels safe enough. He needs an arrangement which permits almost instant hospitalization of the patient, should the need arise. At times, even only two or three days of hospitalization can make a crucial difference. This provision certainly helps to give one more therapeutic freedom with less anxiety for patient and therapist. The hospital provides some immediate protection for the patient and gives the therapist freedom to engage in interventions which might possibly be upsetting to the patient.

Though therapeutic freedom sometimes has to include interventions which might prove unnerving to the patient, I do not believe in inducing regressions intentionally: I am not certain that therapeutically induced regressions and dissociations may not lay the foundation for easier regression and dissociation at other times, and therefore do not consider them a desirable therapeutic modality.

However, I do believe in such active steps as cathartic interpretations, i.e. interpreting unconscious material directly à la John Rosen (1962), without waiting until it becomes preconscious, as is more customary in the treatment of less disturbed people.

Aside from the importance of having easy access to a hospital, it is extremely desirable that it be a hospital setting in which one can continue to see and treat one's own patient while he is there. This type of situation is often difficult to attain because teaching hospitals always insist on having only their residents and staff treat patients. In view of this fact, proprietary hospitals, which may be otherwise less desirable, are to be preferred. While the patient is hospitalized for an acute disorder, actively deluded and hallucinated, one can make crucial interventions which will speed up the therapeutic process greatly. Of course, it is also essential that the patient has a sense of not being deserted, so it is extremely beneficial when there is continuity of contact. Therefore, anyone who wants to engage frequently in the treatment of acutely disturbed psychotics has to cultivate a close relationship with a hospital that will permit him quick hospitalization and continued care of his own patient, both psychotherapeutically as well as psychopharmacologically.

Another aspect which may be even more difficult than the first two with regard to hospitalization is that it must be possible to get one's patients released from the hospital as promptly as possible. Ordinarily, administrative procedures may make it difficult to remove a patient from the hospital speedily. Yet, those patients who are suitable for ambulatory psychotherapy could especially easily be harmed by excessively long hospitalization which induces passivity and secondary gains from the hot-house conditions of support and external controls.

4) *A Family Network*

This point is really an elaboration of the second one, namely the requirement that there be at least one person whom the therapist can address himself to, who will take some responsibility for the patient. If there is a whole *family network* available, this may play a crucial and beneficial role. Family network therapy has a definite and well-known place in treatment. Especially if inter-family pathology plays a marked role, it is essential to draw other family members into the therapeutic situation. This may be accomplished in different ways. Indeed, one may choose to engage in either conjoint therapy with one other family member, or in family therapy per se. Under certain circumstances, the original therapist may wish to work with the entire family himself. In other instances, it may be more suitable to have other family members, or even the entire family, seen by another psychiatrist or social worker or psychologist. The two therapists must have the privilege of conferring with each other, so as to work as a team, even if not necessarily under the same roof.

5) *An Auxiliary Therapist*

The above point brings me to one of the less well-known and less practiced techniques, and that is the desirability of utilizing an *auxiliary therapist,* i.e. having two therapists treating the same patient simultaneously. The auxiliary therapist may be drawn in only during particularly stormy episodes. These may be due to an especially acute transference psychosis, or at times to a particular countertransference problem on the part of the therapist. Then the role of the auxiliary therapist is to deal specifically with the transference psychotic phenomenon which may be too difficult for the patient, and maybe for the primary therapist, to handle directly. Meanwhile, the primary therapist continues to work on the problems that produced the acute transference psychosis.

Dyadic psychotherapy, especially in an office, can be a very lonely type of endeavor, fraught with all sorts of emotions, including anxiety for both therapist and patient. Therefore, it is often very useful to have, as a routine proviso, an auxiliary therapist who can dilute the transference and countertransference, if necessary. If one routinely works with acutely disturbed psychotics, it is often useful to introduce an auxiliary therapist early in the relationship, explaining to the patient that this colleague will be available should the primary therapist catch a cold, go on vacation, or otherwise be unavailable. Such availability, of course, is crucially important with the most highly disturbed people. This kind of arrangement is made more easily in a clinic or social agency than in private practice, but it is not impossible in the latter.

6) *Awareness of Family and Community Resources*

Especially for psychiatrists in private practice, it is important to be aware of all possible *resources in a patient's life* (relatives, friends, etc.) *and in the community.* Social workers and psychologists are more likely to be aware of these social support systems, such as social agencies, rehabilitation facilities, halfway houses, recreational facilities, and eventually vocational rehabilitation. It is important to make use of these facilities during treatment and certainly towards the end of treatment, when the patient needs a setting in which he can continue his improvement and recovery.

7) *Hot-lines and Emergency Centers*

A variation on the theme of having access to an auxiliary therapist is the need to have easy access to *hot-lines and emergency centers.* Most communities, at this point, do have such services available, as part of their community facilities. These emergency services are usually listed on the inside cover of the phone book and, when they are properly administered, are accessible 24 hours a day. The telephone contact should be backed up by an available psychiatric emergency center in a clinic or social agency and, if possible, a mobile team which can visit a patient in his home and, in an extreme situation, commit and hospitalize him.

8) *Do Not Be a Hero*

I consider it extremely important to have *easy access to an alarm system,* in case a patient should become acutely disturbed and possibly dangerous. The ability to treat acutely disturbed people depends as much on the relative security of the setting within which therapy takes place, as on the therapist's capacity to tolerate feelings of anxiety and discomfort. Under any circumstances, *it is essential not to be inappropriately heroic.* The therapist should never allow situations to exist which are unduly dangerous in terms of his own safety. An anxious therapist can certainly not function effectively. An unsecured setting also makes the patient uneasy, because he may well fear his own possible loss of impulse control. Especially in large and active emergency treatment centers, it is best to have security personnel available. In settings which are less likely to have extremely disturbed patients, it is advantageous to have an office which is not located in too isolated a setting. It may be helpful to leave the door slightly ajar, provided that reasonable privacy is still retained. Again, such a provision is often also of benefit to the patient, who feels less frightened of the therapist and of his own impulses, when he perceives the situation as relatively secure.

9) *Housing Situations*

This point deals with a very difficult problem—the *suitability of the patient's housing situation*: namely, where the patient lives and where he or she should live for optimal improvement. The family setting is often extremely unhealthy and it may be almost impossible to do constructive therapeutic work in two or three hours a week if the remainder of the time there are forces within the family setting which are regressive and pathogenic. Therefore, it is often essential, and certainly a major enabling condition, that if his present living situation is unsuitable then the patient must be moved to another setting. At first glance, this often appears to be impossible. I strongly suggest a very careful survey of all his relatives, friends and community resources, in an attempt to find a place for the patient to live and to sleep other than with his immediate family, if they are acutely pathogenic. If there are no appropriate relatives or friends, then foster homes or even half-way houses may be preferable, even though these facilities are often deleterious in their own way.

I cannot stress strongly enough the importance of proper living situation for the patient, in order not to have the therapeutic process be more difficult than is necessary, or even to be ineffective. I have found this factor, namely a healthy setting, to be so important, that if a patient of mine had a suitable family member living in another state, I was in favor of the patient moving to that other state, living with that family, and continuing with another therapist rather than myself.

10) *Drugs*

Finally, the use of *drugs* has to be mentioned as one very important enabling condition for engaging in psychotherapy with acutely disturbed psychotic patients. Medication may enable the doctor to engage in the often painful but necessary interventions, and still have a cooperative patient. Interpretations may be extremely painful and distressing for a patient—indeed, more than he can bear. This may provoke an episode of violence to himself or others, and lead to a more acute psychotic state. In other instances, without the benefit of psychotropic medication, the patient may be generally too anxious, too withdrawn, or too depressed to be either willing or able to communicate. Some patients may be terrified of approaching particular subject matters, material which it is crucial to air and analyze. In such instances, drugs can be used to decrease "approach anxiety" or, as in the case of antidepressants, provide the patient with the "energy" to relate.

Caution must be observed not to medicate a patient to a point where most ego functions are interfered with and reality testing and the sense of self have been unduly affected by the psychotropic drug (Bellak, Hurvich & Gediman, 1973). It is undesirable to have a patient who feels foggy or "spaced-out"—so lethargic as not to have any motivation for psychotherapeutic work. But it is, in fact, possible to choose one's drugs in such a way that some ego functions are improved, thereby facilitating the therapeutic process. Improvement of impulse control, e.g. of aggression, may be accomplished with lithium or phenothiazines. The latter may also improve thought processes, helping the patient to think logically and reason deductively—skills basic to his understanding therapeutic interpretations.

SUMMARY

Before initiating ambulatory therapy with acutely disturbed psychotics, it is not only necessary to make a diagnosis in the narrow sense of the word, but also extremely important to evaluate all assets and liabilities in the patient's life situation. All difficulties which are likely to emerge in the process of treatment should be carefully assessed and planned for (Bellak & Meyers, 1975). Such accurate assessment and treatment design can serve to eliminate a great deal of trouble, waste and even tragedy.

However, if at least the minimal enabling conditions outlined above are met, the ambulatory treatment of acutely disturbed psychotics may be a truly rewarding experience for both patient and therapist. In most instances, after the acute condition has been dealt with, it is desirable to engage in extensive psychoanalytic psychotherapy in order to deal with the patient's subtle structural, dynamic and characterological problems.

REFERENCES

BELLAK, L., HURVICH, M., and GEDIMAN, H. *Ego Functions in Schizophrenics, Neurotics, and Normals. A Systematic Study of Conceptual, Diagnostic, and Therapeutic Aspects.* New York: John Wiley & Sons, 1973.

BELLAK, L. and MEYERS, B. Ego function assessment and analysability. *The International Review of Psycho-Analysis*, 1975, 2:413-427.

ROSEN, J. *Direct Psychoanalytic Psychiatry.* New York: Grune & Stratton, 1962.

II. Intrinsic Problems

The analyst or therapist who faces no problems or crises in his practice has managed to take on only relatively healthy patients and to avoid the very sick. He is like a physician of whom it was said, "He is a doctor for the healthy; God help the sick!"

As is true of other medical specialties, not everyone responds to treatment equally well. Some patients have chronic illnesses for which there is no cure. For these patients prolonged symptomatic and supportive therapy preserves a marginal level of function and fends off periodic exacerbations as much as possible. Other patients follow an inexorable course of progressive deterioration despite heroic efforts and measures. Some situations become very dire. Occasionally, a patient commits suicide. Certainly, psychotic decompensations are sometimes unavoidable.

When the therapist is dealing with such catastrophic situations, as most therapists must, he often needs to remind himself that, as dedicated as he may be to being helpful to the patient, if things really go badly, no one can be expected to be a miracle worker. This holds true for psychiatry as well as any other medical specialty. After he has assured himself that he has attained as much knowledge and experience as possible and has done all he can, he has no reason for self-recriminations.

8. Panic

Panic may occur in the patient during the analytic or therapeutic process because of the emergence of uncontrollable conflicts. The patient may develop symptoms such as diaphoresis, tachycardia, hyperventilation, tremors, dizziness, blurred vision, chest pain, etc., and suffer from a feeling of impending disaster and, at times, the fear that he is "going crazy." This cluster of symptoms, like a fever with night sweats, shaking and chills when one is physically sick, is a *nonspecific* response to a specific pathological process.

The management of anxiety can take several forms. The use of anxiolytic medication may be indicated. Its use may be compared to prescribing aspirin in order to avoid the damaging effects of *excessive* hyperpyrexia. (Fever which is not dangerously high may play a constructive role in terms of killing off infectious organisms in the body, just as *tolerable* anxiety promotes the psychotherapeutic process.) Excessive anxiety or panic increases the patient's resistance to the analytic process as a form of "approach anxiety," i.e., an anticipatory response which leads to avoidance of any issue that might produce further anxiety. Supportive verbal interventions may serve to decrease the extreme intensity of the dysphoria associated with panic. A truly etiological ministration (comparable to the administration of selected antibiotics for a fever induced by a specific infectious agent) involves the interpretation and working-through of specific emotional conflicts. In order to make the appropriate interventions, the therapist must establish the cause of the panic (he

89

must identify the noxious agent) in the context of the individual patient's history and current experiences.

Certain familiar recurrent patterns occur as the sources of anxiety, e.g., *loss of control over impulses,* whether sexual and/or aggressive, *anniversary reactions, separations and/or losses* (real or perceived), *severe superego reactions* following sexual or aggressive activity. Anxiety may also be associated with *inappropriate fears of pregnancy or venereal disease, moral masochism, sudden losses in self-esteem,* and *depersonalizing experiences.* In addition, free-floating panic without manifest content is not infrequent.

It is certainly correct for the therapist to be human with the patient and offer reassurance. In fact, it may be absolutely necessary to do so in order to be able to continue to work with him or her. First, it is crucial to inform him that what is happening to him occurs to other people too. Most patients are convinced that they are the only ones to have such feelings. Secondly, one must demonstrate clearly to the patient a continuity between the immediate *panic,* the *precipitating factors* and *life history.* This gives the patient at least some feeling of control over what seems frighteningly ego-alien.

The analyst should review for himself the material from the several sessions preceding the patient's panic, as well as recent life events, to see whether a significant occurrence or trend can be identified, and to ascertain how the current crisis situation fits in with the analytic work. The analyst should be able to relate the panic to the chief complaint which originally brought the patient into treatment, and in turn relate this chief complaint (along with current panic) to the patient's life history. In this way he can see what similar constellation of forces, either internal or external, existed at these various points in time and gain the needed perspective on the current panic. For example, a patient has a history which includes the death of a parent at an early age. This traumatic event has sensitized her to loss. She later suffers a severe depression when a boyfriend breaks up with her. This is experienced as a repetition of the original trauma—she feels abandoned and helpless as she did at the age of five or whenever the original loss occurred. After several months of treatment, when all has been going well, the patient is suddenly in a panic. Three sessions previous, the therapist informed the patient that he would be leaving for a vacation. Again, the precipitating factor is anticipated or actual separation from an important figure, which reawakens the feelings of helplessness and panic associated with the original loss.

There are a number of dynamic patterns which are the principal causes of panic:

1) Fear of loss of impulse control, whether of an aggressive or sexual nature.

2) Anniversary reactions, most often manifested as a depression, but sometimes presenting as panics and psychotic states. There is excellent statistical evidence that a significant number of people enter a psychiatric hospital on an anniversary date.

3) Separation anxiety, especially in the individual who needs symbiotic relationships. In the analytic context, this panic may be due to separation from the analyst, as in "weekend anxiety" or "vacation anxiety."

4) Drugs, such as marijuana, LSD, or amphetamines, may induce altered states of mind, flashbacks, and consequent acute panic states. Occasionally, a drug such as the phenothiazines will induce panic as a paradoxical reaction. Such feelings of loss of control due to the felt effect of the drug also sometimes occur with the fast-acting barbiturates.

5) Severe superego reactions in response to increased sexual or aggressive feelings and behaviors. This may take various forms, such as the fear of pregnancy, the fear of venereal disease, or a free-floating panic without manifest content.

6) Moral masochism, of which a success neurosis is one aspect. Any new attainment, including therapeutic progress, takes on a forbidden oedipal meaning which is then responded to with panic. This may happen to people who have made a major advance or any marked improvement in any area in their lives. If it occurs in response to therapeutic progress, we call it a "negative therapeutic response."

7) A sudden decrease in self-esteem. In the long run this may lead to a depression and, under certain circumstances, a manic disorder. The first phenomenon at the onset of a psychosis will be a panic. Some neurotic people, on the

other hand, have frequent panics that are *not* a transitional phenomena to a more severe disorder.

8) *Depersonalization* is usually an outgrowth of unacceptable feelings of aggression of one part of the self against another part of the self. Jacobson (1971) points out that if the aggression emanates from the superego and is directed toward the self, the patient will suffer principally from feelings of guilt.

9) *Derealization,* even in such mild fear as déjà vu, may also produce secondary panic by the very nature of the subjective experience.

Many people go into and come out of panics with great ease. Using the current psychological evaluation technique of *ego function assessment* (see Chapter 3), people can be rated on four different levels: 1) current functioning; 2) optimal functioning; 3) characteristic functioning; and 4) subcharacteristic functioning or minimal functioning. Some people have a rather wide spread between their optimum and minimum functioning, while others have a very narrow one. This spread appears to be a basic personality characteristic, similar to what Allport (1937) would have thought of as a trait, i.e., volatility versus stability. Therefore, some people panic easily and also swing back easily, while for others the opposite holds true, i.e., there is little deviation from their characteristic level of functioning.

An example of a patient with a ready inclination to panic is a woman who had a symbiotic relationship with her mother which resulted in her having an acute need for high stimulus input. She required the environment and others to provide her with constant feedback, support input, attention, and nurturance, as her mother had. The mother died in the patient's adolescence and she fled into marriage. It was humanly impossible to provide her with the degree of stimulus input she wanted and needed. Without this high level of input, she had a chronic feeling of emptiness. In the course of her analysis, there were frequent and stormy transference situations with a great deal of affect. When confronted with the limits of reality, she would describe a feeling that a "cardiac lobotomy" was being performed on her, that she was being made affectless. She was afraid to accept the possibility of settling down with her husband, and accepting the reality of some degree of contentment. She was fearful of giving up her wishes for the *high input* she was accustomed to receiving from her mother. The patient was prone to panics and claustrophobic attacks. She perceived the bearing and raising of children as a narcissistic threat, and she was reluctant to give up her notion of a romantic male figure, a fantasy which her husband did not fulfill. The continuity between her perceptions of her current life experiences and past experiences had to be established to lessen the irrational threat which an acceptance of her present situation posed.

Clinically, the analyst may see patients with panics that vary in frequency and intensity. At one end of the spectrum, some patients seem to have no tolerance for anxiety; others have a relatively high tolerance where only infrequent and isolated precipitating events break through defenses. At the extreme end of the spectrum are those patients who are apathetic, where there is no anxiety and the major therapeutic task is to produce a panic or at least anxiety.

The intensity of the panic may range from mild to severe, often depending on the particular psychological meaning of the precipitating event. For example it may be quite severe in the patient who loses his job if his entire identity is defined by his work. The severity of almost any psychiatric condition or crisis will in large part depend on how well the patient functioned prior to the current special situation or crisis.

EXOGENOUS PANIC

A panic resulting from events outside the analytic situation, such as threatening illnesses, job loss, death of a loved one, etc., is, strictly speaking, an exogenous panic. The first principle in dealing with an exogenous panic is to *understand the meaning of the particular precipitating event to this particular person* in terms of his personal history and his perception or apperceptive distortion of the event. This is not to say that external realities which are anxiety-producing should be dismissed, but rather that the intrapsychic contributions (the irrational fears, unresolved conflicts, etc.) leading to a panic state should be identified. Accomplishing this, the analyst has effectively converted the exogenous condition to an endogenous one. The converted exogenous-to-endogenous panic can then be dealt with psychotherapeutically, according to the general methods discussed above and the specific methods discussed below (see Management).

The analyst can employ certain techniques to help make the panic ego-alien. He may say, "Yes, this is a terrible situation. But, I believe if we asked ten people who have had similar experiences, they would most likely react quite differently from you." By this means the analyst can drive a wedge between the strictly subjective experience of panic and introduce some objectivity. This distancing also aids the process of converting the panic from an exogenous to endogenous panic. The endogenous factor, the unconscious conflict or fear causing irrational anxiety or panic will have a disorganizing effect on the patient's mental functioning in proportion to the brittleness of the patient's premorbid personality.

In summary, with an exogenous panic, part of the analyst's job is to immediately make the experience ego-alien by emphasizing that many other people have had similar experiences with less resulting anxiety and to explore the patient's particular reaction in the context of the specific panic-inducing situation and in the broader context of his history, preexisting conflicts and set of apperceptive distortions.

MANAGEMENT

In dealing with crises, psychotherapists try to establish formulas, parameters, and methods of organization which can help the patient. Depending on the nature of the panic and the specific characteristics of the patient, the analyst's interventions may range from nondirective ones to drastic and extensive procedures. In some cases, if the therapist chooses the course of minimal intervention, it may encourage the patient to break off treatment because the panic situation is unbearable for him.

Be Available

The first rule that the analyst needs to follow in a panic situation is to make himself available to the patient. Although the transference problems and secondary gains of this loss of analytic distance will require analyzing later on, the therapist's first consideration is to save the patient.

If the patient calls in the middle of the night in a panic, the analyst should simply listen for a while, until he understands the nature of the panic. He must ascertain exactly the patient's physical surroundings and availability of others: Is he in a strange place? A public place? Is he in bed at home with the lights on? Is there someone with him or someone in close proximity? A friend who can be called? etc. Then, the analyst can engage in some interventions. Talking with the patient over the phone, he can offer support and sometimes insight. Being alone will increase the patient's panic; the analyst must urge him to stay with another person for a while. The patient should be asked to call the analyst again after he has called in another member of the household or has arrived at the home of a friend or relative. This show of interest on the analyst's part will help the patient enormously. This intervention must be followed up by an appointment made for the earliest possible date.

Whatever the analyst does outside the usual analytic procedure to help the patient in a panic must, in due course, be analyzed and re-analyzed as to its causes and effects, sometimes until the end of treatment. If, for example, the patient asks for an extra hour of analysis, this may possibly be seen as a form of acting-out. However, in the midst of a panic, it is unsafe to tell the patient that he is acting out. At that time, direct intervention and support are important and appropriate. The deviation from standard analytic technique can always be dealt with later on, and repeatedly if necessary.

Provide a Structure

In a panic situation, almost any structure the therapist can provide is helpful. The first bombings of London during World War II caused havoc. After some very definite rules were established for behavior during bombings, civilian panics virtually disappeared. Furthermore, if adults were panicky during the blitz, children were also. But if the parents were calm, with a definite procedure to follow, the children remained calm too. A patient should be helped to increase signal awareness. Being able to pick up clues that he is beginning to experience anxiety helps him anticipate and avoid a total panic.

When a patient comes to a first session in a panic, the analyst should, as in all crisis situations, deal with the most immediate concerns. He should get to know the patient, obtain a data base which includes the chief complaint, any related complaints, life history, and the precipating factors related to his current panic, as well as the reason for the patient's decision to seek help now. He should review the nature of panic for the patient to try to establish a continuity between the patient's present fears and his past experience, giving the patient a feeling of control over the panic, assuring him that it *can* be handled, that it has *causal connections* and need not be experienced as an alien force, as something beyond his power to understand and work through.

Restructure the Situation

When the realities of the patient's situation precipitate panics or do not provide enough protection against panics, the therapist should suggest that the patient restructure that situation. In one case, a very difficult father repeatedly set off the patient. Analysis was difficult while he was "sitting on a hot stove." In order to deal with the situation, the therapist had to suggest that the patient remove himself from the home for a while.

In the strictly analytic situation, a variation of restructuring the situation occurs when the patient *sits up*. Analysts are reluctant to have the patient do this because it seems like such an "un-analytical" approach. This maneuver, however, often provides needed external validation of how the analyst looks, how he responds to the patient and interacts with him. This lessens the dangers of perceptual isolation and reduces the emergence of threatening primary-process features. However, this tactic will undoubtedly cause some problems in the analysis which will have to be analyzed subsequently.

Another crucial variant of restructuring often involves the unstable patient who *lives alone*. Especially if the therapist is concerned about crippling panics, suicidal danger, and the possibility of psychosis, he must discuss with the patient alternative living arrangements until the panic situation is over. The patient may temporarily live with friends or relatives or, if need be, other provisions, such as brief hospitalization, can be made.

Auxiliary Reality Testing

Part of the analyst's armamentarium is his ability to help the patient plan *realistically* and to provide him with a sense of how *to cope concretely* with his situation. This part of the therapist's job is, of course, in addition to *understanding and interpreting the meaning* of the panic. In fact, the primary emphasis is on the details of analytic interpretation. However, if the panic is unrelieved, the analyst may appropriately become the auxiliary ego, helping the patient plan and reality test.

Along these lines, it is important for the analyst to allow himself to be human. He must recognize when the patient is going through an actual experience of an overwhelming nature (such as in the loss of a loved one or in the acquisition of some dire illness) where a profound emotional reaction is realistic and appropriate. The analyst certainly should be aware of and monitor his own emotional reactions; part of the analyst's countertransference reaction might be to rush in with too much support or with premature interpretations, neither of which is appropriate. In such situations, he need not interpret instantaneously. Rather, he should become concerned only when normal processes turn into pathological ones, for example, if grief becomes melancholia. The analyst should enter into the dynamics included in a patient's reaction to a given situation only when this seems to be specifically called for and such intervention can be helpful. Otherwise, he should just stand by. There is no substitute for tact in any number of situations, especialy exogenous panic. If a patient comes to analysis after a mugging, it is poor technique and poor tact to immediately interpret the patient's passive wishes and point out how the mugging must have reactivated them. A mugging is, after all, a terrifying experience for anyone, and it is only reasonable for an individual who has been mugged to be very upset. Dreams and other material may appear after a few days have passed; at that point there may be occasion to deal with the psychological aspects of the mugging, if the emotional sequelae have become pathological.

REFERENCES

ALLPORT, G. W. *Personality: A Psychological Interpretation*. New York: Henry Holt & Co., 1937.

JACOBSON, E. *Depression: Comparative Studies of Normal, Neurotic, and Psychotic Conditions*. New York: International Universities Press, 1971.

9. Acting-out:
General Propositions

Classical analysts restrict the use of the phrase "acting-out" to behavior that occurs only in analysis, as part of transference manifestations and as a form of resistance in the analytic process. This definition is too narrow. On the other extreme, some use the term for any action of which they disapprove or which they view as socially unacceptable. Consequently, they tend to interpret too many behaviors both in daily life and in analysis as acting-out. This over-inclusive definition overlooks the fact that some behaviors are, after all, just actions—reality-based, with adult motives and goals (though perhaps unconscious), and appropriate to the human condition.

In clinical practice it is useful to view a variety of clearly discernible and often miniscule acts or sets of behaviors, as well as entire character structures and life-styles, as forms of acting-out. This view facilitates the formulation of a reasonable and practical approach to the problems which arise in the course of therapy and the crises they engender.

Forms of Acting-out

Acting-out in the transference includes transference sentiments that are translated into action outside the analysis. For example,

99

genital or pre-genital sexual feelings toward the therapist are expressed in the actual sexual life of the patient with people outside the therapeutic setting (it is important to keep in mind that pregenital feelings may sometimes be disguised as genital).

Defensive acting-out in the transference concerns conflicted transference sentiments which are translated into action outside the analysis. Overeating, for example, may be an expression of a desire to be fed like a small child, as well as an unwillingness to assume adult behavior and adult gratification.

Neurotic acting-out is an unconscious programmed and circumscribed behavioral statement involving specific areas of functioning which are conflictual. For example, in a success neurosis, the attainment of success is equated with the attainment of the forbidden oedipal object and the individual arranges always to fall short of success or perhaps constantly fail. One particular patient had a perfect attendance record at school but was compelled to miss the last day. Another, who had great fears about the harm he might do women, was compelled after intercourse to have a homosexual encounter against the wall of a police station, making the complex statement that for daring to have intercourse with a woman it behooved him to get *himself* "screwed" and, in addition, get caught and punished by the law.

Characterological acting-out involves behaviors representing general statements or attitudes toward life situations and activities now so separated from the original and specific conflictual triggers as to be evoked by diverse stimuli. Adler's (1917) concepts of male and female protest are exemplary visions of such life-styles. The somewhat 19th century view of the female as a tender violet who would turn pale, faint, take sick, etc. when her sensibilities were offended would be an example of the female protest. By such behavior, she would attempt to manipulate others into giving her what she wanted. The male protest, on the other hand, would be the macho-aggressive approach whereby he would strive to achieve his ends by controlling or overriding others by his "brute strength." In Adler's view, such acting-out behaviors also involved a "fictive goal," an imaginary or fantasy goal which motivated such characterological acting-out.

The fictive goal would be a preconscious or unconscious goal on the part of the patient—for example, the desire to seduce father and take him away from mother, or vice versa. Certain popular characters may be viewed as characterological forms of acting-out. Tallulah Bankhead let everyone know she was an *enfant terrible.* Somerset Maugham, a homosexual, reflected his bitter disappointment at the loss of his mother when he was a small boy in both his life and his writing. In *Of Human Bondage* and *Rain,* for example, he dramatically sets forth the theme of the great dangers posed to men who become involved with women. An example of such characterological acting-out in the context of more normal development would be the rebellious adolescent whose feelings are translated into action as an entire life-style. His acting-out may be motivated by his fear of being destroyed as an entity, or may be an attempt to delineate himself clearly by acting in opposition to authority.

Acting-out behaviors may be more intense and/or more frequent as a consequence of certain "organic" states. Children who have delayed neurological development, something akin to dyslexia and minimal brain dysfunction, would be predisposed to acting out their ideas and feelings rather than translating them into language. This is so because they simply do not have the verbal tools available to them. In normally developed individuals, *overstimulation,* acute or chronic, will predispose toward the translation of thoughts and feelings into action. In this case, the acting-out constitutes an overflow mechanism which provides direct tension discharge. Such individuals have an acute or chronic need or tendency to blow off steam. *Some women seem to act out more premenstrually.* The endocrine changes, perhaps affecting mood, the water retention and electrolyte shifts that are irritating to the meninges, the general discomfort from edema and soreness and perhaps some as yet unknown factors may all contribute to the increased propensity to act out during this time. In analysis, as in a marriage, it is important for the partner to know where a woman stands in the menstrual cycle. It should be remembered, however, that some women react with marked mood swings, including aggression and irritability, while others are not affected to any marked degree. If there is any evidence of a disturbed EEG, migraine headaches, or minimal brain dysfunction, the likelihood of behavioral changes premenstrually is also greater.

Acting-out may also occur secondary to major ego function deficits. Greenacre (1950) has stressed that, where there is delayed speech development, there is a tendency to translate thoughts and feelings into action. By two-and-a-half, a child is expected to be able to express himself verbally. He may fail at this task for a number of reasons. Language is a form of communication we usually consider as part of the secondary process which requires a complex set of functions, e.g., a good synthetic function, and the capacity for symbolization and metaphor. The primary process lends itself to direct acting-out rather than to verbal statements.

Greenacre (1950) further speculates that genetic factors may play a role in the predisposition for acting-out. Disturbances in judgment, failure of fusion of primitive ego-nuclei and consequent poor self-boundaries, poor cognitive functions (such as a tendency toward magical thinking) can all be implicated in the phenomenon of acting-out. Even impulsiveness, an inability to tolerate frustration, is suggested by Greenacre as a discrete factor in acting-out.

Finally, although the basic definition of acting-out is the *behavioral* expression of something that should be expressed verbally, there are certain forms of *inappropriate verbalization* that also fit the concept of acting-out. An inappropriate verbalization may have the impulsivity, poor judgment, and programmed nature of behavioral acting-out. For instance, some people will always feel compelled to make verbal statements that pit them against authority. Others, as part of a character disorder, persist in saying things guaranteed to make them look eccentric or odd. Here, verbalizations are the outstanding part of a whole piece of unconsciously programmed behavior.

A Digression

Often forms of acting-out have certain personal or social adaptive aspects. An acting-out person may be unconscious of his motives and, subjectively, his actions may not benefit him; however, in some cases, his acting-out may be socially useful. For instance, the young revolutionary who kills the tyrant has performed an act which may be very beneficial for society. From his standpoint, however, the action may well have been motivated by unconscious aggression toward his father. This kind of acting-out probably happens often. Most social revolutions, for better or for worse, are started by late adolescents. They are acting out their anger against their parents (the older generation), in an unconscious process which is sometimes adaptive when seen from a social perspective.

Many lesser forms of acting-out have direct advantages to the individual. In actors, for example, acting-out may facilitate playing a role, throwing oneself into the part, identifying with the character. Other people who act out in daily life may have more fun than the good bourgeois who goes to work every day and minds his own business. Certain social roles may give aggressive acting-out adaptive features for an individual. "Ba-Ba" Boyington did very well while he was shooting down Korean planes, but after his term in the Air Force he became an alcoholic. He had many reasons for wanting to express his aggression and the Korean war provided the means. However, without this outlet, his aggression found a pathological expression. A patient, a young married woman with conflicted gender identity, left her husband, established a lesbian relationship, and joined her grandfather's large and lucrative construction business, which she eventually came to own. Her behavior can be seen as a form of acting-out-as-character-formation, with adaptive features; she became head of a construction company—a not very common accomplishment for women. Not all acting-out is pathological in the sense of being maladaptive, in a social sense, even though the motivation behind it may be problematic, based on unresolved conflicts or pathological character traits.

ANAMNESIS AND ASSESSMENT

The best indicator of potential acting-out in a patient is a history of acting-out. And the more severe the previous acting-out, the more cautious one should be. For example, a history of the mistreatment or the killing of domestic pets, a very pathological phenomenon, should make one consider the possibility of serious destructive acts toward self or others, even if there are no other alarming indicators. Early history may also reveal inconsistency in an individual's upbringing, for instance, mixed messages from the parents, which facilitates acting-out. Such contradictory signals or messages make the development of synthetic and integrative functions more difficult, and that tends to contribute to acting-out, rather than to foster thinking and verbalization. A mitigating factor in this situation would be the presence of some appropriate guilt or upset in these early acting-out situations. This would indicate the presence of a superego, albeit a somewhat unstable one which may slip occasionally and may be overwhelmed under very provocative circumstances, thus leading to a loss of impulse control. If there is no hint of a guilt, one needs to be all the more concerned.

Finally, history may reveal acting-out hidden behind certain socially appropriate activities which may be highly adaptive for the individual within a specific context, but, at the same time, may be the basis of significant maladaptive behaviors in other circumstances. Such behaviors bode ominously for treatment. Actors, for example, often act off the stage as well as on. This may help them excel in their careers but lead to severely impaired intrapsychic functioning and interpersonal relationships. A soldier is likely to have made aggressive acting-out an adaptive phenomenon within the context of his professional career, but the aggression may be injurious to self and/or others in other circumstances—especially if the individual is deprived of his socially adaptive outlet. A careful review of the history in individual events and episodes in the patient's life, viewed in the overall framework or perspective of the patient's life-style or career choice, will help us establish the likelihood of acting-out in the therapeutic context.

Dynamically, acting-out represents past apperceptions, which (now unconscious), dominate contemporary apperception and are translated into a behavioral statement. The *defenses* employed under such circumstances tend to be *primarily denial* and *secondarily repression,* thus making the acting-out ego-syntonic rather than ego-alien. The bizarre or extreme behaviors which people may manifest and maintain as ego-syntonic are sometimes amazing. Acting-out also implies poor *ego functions,* above all, poor *impulse control* and *poor judgment.* Typically, people who are acting out may be vaguely aware that they may not be doing the best or wisest thing; however, at the same time, there is the feeling that, in this special situation, the behavior makes sense, is justifiable or a good thing to do. Under such circumstances there is a definite defect in judgment under the impact of very urgent impulses. The hallmarks of acting-out are *urgency* and *impulsivity.* To quote Greenacre (1950), "The impulsiveness is based on an inability to tolerate frustration, a special disturbance of reality and of self-criticism, the quality of marked motility or activity often of a dramatic character—all especially characteristic of extremely severe neuroses which sometimes appear close to psychoses and psychopathies." Again, this resembles what Glover called different ego-nuclei which never quite merge; thus, whole isolated ego states are translated into often disruptive action rather than having been synthesized into an integrated affect or character trait which can be expressed verbally. Mary O'Neill Hawkins* described such patients (often hysterical) as suffering from "permanently fluctuating stable states." They come in one day with one set of emotions and beliefs, and in the next session come in with a totally different, but equally ardent, set of attitudes and feelings, not even recalling that the others existed. What seemed of prime importance at one time is simply ignored or obliterated later on. The Grande Hysterics, such as fugue states and multiple personalities, are extreme forms of such ego states which emerge independently, presented as a Dr. Jekyll and Mr. Hyde character in the most romantic tradition. In such cases, acting-out is a splitting off of a part of the self; one part of the self is acted out and the other part is repressed, with a simultaneous failure of the synthetic function.

REFERENCES

Adler, A. *The Neurotic Constitution.* New York: Moffat, Yard, 1917.
Greenacre, P. General problems of acting out. *Psychoanal. Quart.,* 19:455, 1950.

---

* Personal communication.

10. Acting-out: General Management

GENERAL MEASURES

Minor forms of acting-out can usually be handled by such ordinary techniques as interpretation. However, the more severe forms require special consideration. The latter seriously threaten the course of psychoanalytic treatment. The management of acting-out will obviously vary from patient to patient, but the therapist may consider the following general short-range procedures.

Interpretation

Interpretation is *the* "royal" form of intervention, whenever indicated and possible. What is required here is for the analyst to understand the meaning of a particular form of acting-out, formulate it for the patient, find common denominators and other occasions of acting-out, and especially relate the contemporary acting-out to childhood events. One can hope to make unconscious, nonverbalized sentiments conscious and verbally manageable and, by such means, avoid future acting-out.

Cathartic Interpretation

If acting-out is defined as a translation of ideational content into behavior that has a circumscribed programatic nature (i.e., patient

106

behaves in such a way that A will lead to B, and B will lead to C), then a cathartic interpretation, an interpretation of otherwise inaccessible unconscious material, may have a definite beneficial effect. This material may need considerable discussion, however. Cathartic interpretation may be facilitated if the analyst presents things very concretely to the patient. This will help make clear the unconscious meaning of the patient's acting-out. Such an interpretation may require a great deal of repetition before it is effective.

Some patients have families where the style of communication is very concrete and involves little verbalization, little exchange of abstract ideas. In such a situation the therapist can avoid actually having to teach the patient to verbalize if, instead, he very specifically points out the common denominators between the behavior in which the patient is currently involved and what was *done to him* in the past. For example, the patient was frustrated by having insufficient communication with his parents. He felt rejected or neglected and thus gives others in his current life "the silent treatment." He "pays back" others for what he was made to suffer. Elsewhere I have said that "Man's inhumanity to man is revenge for the indignities suffered in childhood" (Bellak, 1970). For example, if the patient is a father who beats his child, chances are that the analyst can point out that this is exactly what the patient's father did to him. Technically, this form of acting-out is identification with the aggressor and accounts for much of human misery. Studies of top Nazi leaders strongly indicate that, in essence, and unconsciously, they were repaying everyone for what was done to them as children.

Cathartic interpretations are especially indicated in acting-out. Ordinarily, we interpret only after material has become preconscious and hope to promote a situation in which the patient is then able to have conscious insight into the preconscious patterns. Typically, we prepare the patient for an interpretation by "focusing" and making a variety of preparatory statements, and either expect the patient to find the common denominator, the insight, himself, or wait until the patient has enough partial insights so that the therapist only has to put a few finishing touches in the form of a well-formulated interpretation.

In distinction, cathartic interpretation is the pointing out of common denominators which are still *entirely* unconscious to the patient. One goes directly to the heart of the matter without preparation. If this is done appropriately and all works well, the patient has a very sudden "Aha" experience, a very powerful affective one, possibly accompanied by crying or symptom laughter. Catharsis takes place, frequently with an immediate cessation of acting-out.

Bargain for a Delay

When acting-out is an isolated defense, particularly to some point of transference, the cathartic interpretation may have some dangers. The analyst should then suggest or arrange for a delay of the acting-out. He can say, for example, "That may be how you feel now, but I suggest that you hold off and give the situation more consideration." Once the analyst is able to get the acting-out patient to put off the behavior, he may well lose all interest in acting-out. The acting-out will then lack the magical appeal because the immediate impulse discharge has been eliminated.

Make the Behavior Ego-Alien

The analyst can point out to the patient that he is almost forced, by his past history, to repeat his actions. Being thus programmed deprives him of freedom of choice. This intervention will often take away much of the fun involved in acting-out. A good deal of the pleasure of acting-out is the gratification of the impulse to do what one wants when one wants. Removal of the *narcissistic pleasure,* as well as the *magical implications,* is achieved by explanations and clarifications of the programmed nature of the activity. Mental health is often defined as "having a choice." The more disturbed the patient, the more he will be a programmed organism. The more stable the personality, the greater the degree of freedom he will enjoy.

Strengthen the Superego

The analyst can strengthen the acting-out patient's superego by pointing out the consequences of his acting-out. For example, with a suicidal patient one might point out that taking her own life will not only severely damage her younger child but will also terribly disturb her husband and parents.

Strengthening Ego Functions

The therapist can ally himself with the healthy part of the patient's ego by saying, for example, "One part of you is programmed irrationally and another part of you is an intelligent, rational adult. The intelligent, rational adult in you and I (the therapist) have to work together to prevent the programmed irrational part of you from engaging in routinized behavior which occurs whenever certain cues appear."

Of course, strengthening of the ego functions in a variety of ways is also indicated. In effect, when we interpret acting-out we engage in auxiliary reality testing and try to improve the judgment of the patient so as to affect his impulse control. We interfere especially with the defenses of denial and repression and sometimes of projection. We encourage the autonomous functions by facilitating verbalization rather than expression of thought and feeling through behavior. We try to augment synthetic functions by reviewing again and again the unconscious motives behind the patient's acting-out and tying together for him dissociative events by interpretive statements.

Positive and Negative Reinforcement

The analyst should suggest to the patient every time he acts out that he is reinforcing the destructive behavior pattern once again. However, every time he refrains from acting-out, he helps eradicate the previous conditioning and reinforces more adaptive behavior. By this method the analyst can establish a subtle system of rewards for not acting out and, by inference, bad marks for acting-out behaviors.

Prediction

One of the most effective ways to deal with acting-out is to systematically and intentionally predict for the patient under what circumstances he is likely to act out. By getting the specific details of events surrounding the acting-out, the analyst can usually find clues as to what precipitates the process of acting-out and can clearly predict that the patient will behave the same way again when he encounters the same situation. The analyst, of course, couches this in hopes that his prediction will turn out to be wrong. This increases signal awareness of cues that are likely to forewarn acting-out, and such awareness, combined with making the behavior ego-alien, will obviate the need for acting-out.

Remove the Patient from the Pathogenic Situation

If a patient habitually places himself in a situation which endangers his life, his livelihood, or his general state of affairs, the analyst must take active steps to prevent this behavior. He does not always have the luxury of waiting for the right interpretation to bring about eventual change. He must suggest that the patient change his work situation so that the acting-out will be decreased or eliminated. A clinical example is that of a male patient in early adolescence who is sleeping with his mother. This must lead to acting-out on his part, be it homosexual, heterosexual, or violent behavior. It will be almost impossible to deal with this problem analytically as long as he continues to sleep with his mother. In many cases, the patient lives in a situation which chronically provides overstimulation. The acting-out under these circumstances is an attempt to "blow off steam." The analyst acts as the patient's auxiliary reality tester, pointing out what triggers the acting-out, and takes a very active role in changing the setting.

Prohibition

Prohibition is rarely used in contemporary psychoanalysis or psychotherapy, but in acting-out behavior it may still have its place. There is very little control we have over our patients. Therefore, prohibition is not easily made effective. It is best used by coupling it with pointing out possible dire consequences of acting-out behavior and saying that therefore the patient should not do such and such.

The only ultimate threat a therapist has, which must be used sparingly, is saying that, if the patient persists in a particular behavior, there is no point in continuing the therapy, and that it will have to be terminated. Of course, this intervention is not indicated if part of the function of acting-out is precisely the one of interrupting therapy.

Enlist the Help of Others

At times, the therapeutic armamentarium alone is not sufficient. This may hold true with suicidal or assaultive patients, as well as with some acting-out ones. It is important in all instances to know precisely who in the patient's life could be called upon to help, if necessary. I therefore strongly suggest that at the beginning of treatment one get the names and addresses of such people who might play a helpful role in the patient's life—just in case serious problems should come up in the course of treatment.

Sometimes there are relatively undramatic life situations where there is a need to interfere with harmful acting-out. In one instance, a college student with a marked success neurosis was going to fail to graduate because he was simply frightened of taking his examinations. At the time it seemed crucial for him to graduate. Neither interpretation nor drug treatment enabled him to cope with this crippling anxiety, which was a form of acting out his success neurosis. I therefore engaged the help of his fiancée and asked her to walk him to the examination room. This she did, but we soon discovered that as soon as she left the room he would also leave, sometimes by another door, while she had thought she had accomplished her task. I finally had to ask her to sit right next to him while he was taking the examination. This was sufficient to keep him there and allow him to pass. Later on, we could analyze his problems at more leisure. Later still, he graduated successfully from engineering school, and judging from communications every few years, he is doing well. If he had been permitted to fail at the time, I believe it would have seriously affected the course of his life. Possibly he would never have graduated from college as a result of his particular conflicts.

Medications

Drugs can be useful at times and under certain circumstances when the patient is likely to act out. The more disturbed the patient, the more reasonable the use of drugs. Especially in the analytic treatment of psychotics, it may be wise to have them on a drug until the accumulated anxiety or aggression that might trigger acting-out can be controlled. If a patient is experiencing premenstrual tension or a migraine headache with visual symptoms, dizziness, nausea, etc., the use of a drug like Dilantin (diphenylhydantoin) is indicated and may help avoid explosive acting-out. Minor tranquilizers and sometimes sedation are helpful in coping with anxiety and facilitating the use of extant ego functions. At times, phobic behavior can be promptly controlled by means of anti-anxiety drugs, enabling the patient, for instance, to use the subway to get to his job despite a subway phobia or to ride in elevators, crucial to his job as a salesman. Later, we can utilize psychotherapy to deal with his problems more basically.

Group Therapy

Group therapy can be useful in addition to individual therapy for treating acting-out behavior. Group feedback may reinforce insight achieved in one-to-one therapy; in some cases, where there is poor impulse control, peer pressure may be helpful.

REFERENCE

BELLAK, L. *The Porcupine Dilemma.* New York: C.P.S., Inc. 1970, 1976.

11. Acting-out: Specific Types and Their Management

Since acting-out is one of the major problems leading to various emergencies in the therapeutic situation, and since, in fact, the therapeutic situation itself invites acting-out, the specific forms of this behavior common to the process need to be considered in detail.

NOT TALKING

Often a patient will not talk in therapy as a form of acting-out. There are many different causes of prolonged silence that are unique to particular patients. For example, one patient lay on the couch for a long while and had great difficulty relating anything at all. This was not a conscious protest. She was reacting to her inability to see the therapist's face from her position on the couch. Her statement was, in essence, "I will not talk because I cannot see how your face reacts to what I am saying, the way I could always tell how my mother felt by looking at her." When this was understood and interpreted, communication improved. More dramatically, another patient related a dream in which she was on a toilet defecating, while the analyst was observing her through the keyhole. With this dream it became apparent that she thought that what she had to say in analysis was pretty dirty stuff, like feces; therefore, talking would be like defecating right there in the office, and this notion made communication impossible for her.

113

In some patients, talking takes on the meaning of submission, opening up and letting the analyst in. The patient perceives talking as a passive process and communication becomes difficult. A more disturbed patient may feel that, by giving away information about himself, he is actually giving away pieces of himself, causing him much anxiety. One such patient reported that, after sessions when he *did* communicate, his situation was getting worse, that he was getting weaker, and that the therapist was only doing things for himself and not for the patient. This paranoid feeling had to be worked through again and again to permit the patient to continue to express himself.

On the other hand, some patients maintain the fantasy that the analyst should understand everything that is on their minds without expressing themselves verbally. This can usually be traced back to a symbiotic relationship with the mother, where much communication occurred through nonverbal cues. The feeling developed that others can divine every wish. Out of such a narcissistic-magic notion, the patient feels that talking should not be necessary in analysis either.

Interventions for Not Talking

It is a technical mistake for the analyst to bear with silence for hours, weeks, months, or years. Very often silence on the patient's part will lead to the breaking off of the treatment because the patient's anxiety and rage increase, as he begins to consider analysis a waste of his time and resources. The analyst must act quickly before the situation becomes unbearable for both. The analyst can help the patient by a variety of means. Changing the patient's position from the couch to the chair, or vice versa, may make it easier for him to talk, even if the situation becomes conversational for a while. Sometimes it is useful for the therapist to repeat for the patient the basic concept of free association. To start off, he can have the patient call off even single words that occur to him. Occasionally, it is useful to suggest to the patient that he has a blank wall in front of him and ask him to "Create a picture on that wall."

This is like using a blank TAT card. The patient will create a mental picture and the analyst can ask him to tell a story about it. This will often indicate to the analyst what is going on in the patient's mind, what he is avoiding, and why he is unable to talk.

The patient's silence will create rage not only in him, but in the analyst as well. The analyst may feel like a fraud in terms of receiving payment from such a patient. The worst approach to such an impasse is for the analyst to remain silent during the patient's prolonged silence. This can be a form of sulking on the analyst's part, an acting-out of the countertransference feelings. If the analyst understands what the silence is about and has specific *reason* to remain silent himself, it is important for him to be human with the patient and at least communicate something like: "I'm sorry it is so difficult for you to talk. I'm sure you have your own reasons and perhaps there are some of which you are not yet aware. I have some thoughts about your difficulty, but I think it would be helpful for a start if you yourself can reach some greater understanding of what keeps you quiet."

A cautionary note: Some patients remain silent because they are depressed. This is *not* a form of acting-out, but rather, a symptom of the depression. In such a case, the analyst must treat the depression with the appropriate means—interpretation, medication, etc.

CRYING

Some patients will spend the analytic hour crying. This must be considered a form of acting-out, in that the patient makes no verbal statement, but instead, a behavioral statement. The best one can usually infer is that the crying is meant to convey the following sentiments: "I feel miserable, I need help," and possibly, "I feel angry," or "I want sympathy." However, as with other nonverbal statements, it is general, lacks precision, is not conceptualized, and is not the optimal form of communication. It may, indeed, represent a preverbal stage of communication.

Therapeutic intervention with this type of acting-out requires special tact. After waiting a certain period of time, five minutes or so, allowing for the fact that the patient *might really need* to cry, the therapist could say: "I'm sorry you feel so bad, but that's all you're communicating to me. As an intelligent person, I feel you can tell me more specifically what's troubling you by talking to me, rather than just crying. While one part of you feels like a child who just wants to cry, I am sure the adult intelligent part of you wants to put the time we have to as much use as possible, so try to tell me what's going on." This technique will make the behavior ego-alien and stress the therapeutic alliance with the healthy part of the personality.

FALLING ASLEEP

Typically, the patient who falls asleep during therapy is orally regressed to a marked degree. He perceives the couch as something akin to his mother's bosom and feels very comfortable there. This type of patient can be seen in terms of Lewin's (1950) oral triad: the wish *to sleep,* the wish *to devour* and the wish *to be devoured,* all part of the oral constellation.

Falling asleep may also serve as a resistance in the same way silence may serve as resistance—when one sleeps, one does not talk. With the patient who falls asleep, resistance and the unconscious confounding of the couch with mother need to be interpreted.

THE BORING PATIENT

Our patients are not boring people; the human drama remains interesting if not fascinating. If at any time the patient becomes really boring, if he persists in discussing trivialities, chances are he is exhibiting a form of *transference resistance.*

Therefore, it is time for the therapist to ask himself precisely *what* the patient is resisting. What is he *not* discussing? This is somewhat of a variation on the theme of not talking. In addition to issues of resistance, very often, a patient is experienced as boring because of *countertransference problems.* For instance, a patient may arouse aggression or homosexual anxiety which is too taxing for the therapist. The therapist's response to this anxiety may be one of feeling bored, of allowing his mind to wander, or of feeling tired and sleepy. These devices are all obviously defenses on the part of the therapist and as such must be analyzed as a reaction to one's own countertransference.

In dealing with problems in therapeutic communication, as soon as a patient is experienced as boring, one should ask oneself, "Is the patient's resistance or my own countertransference interfering?" The feeling of being bored should be an alarm signal. It is true that some patients are certainly more interesting than others. However, a particular patient may be boring because he relates only concrete obsessive details or is otherwise shallow in his communication. This should then be pointed out to the patient and interpreted as a form of resistance to dealing with more conflictual issues. If the patient's behavior cannot be dealt with dynamically, it is possible that he may not be suitable for insight psychotherapy, and some other form of therapy may be indicated.

PSEUDO COMMUNICATION

Patients may persistently engage in more or less superficial communication as a form of acting-out and as a form of resistance. Such a patient may be uninteresting and thus this problem may overlap with that of the boring patient; however, this is not always so. Some patients may regale us with fascinating stories which do not relate to their psychological problems; in this way they keep communication on a superficial level.

A specific form of this type of acting-out, so-called *narcissistic reverie,* consists of very pleasurably relating all kinds of life experiences, greatly *libidinizing the process of communication.* There is revelling in the act of reviewing and sharing the experiences, with minimal attempt to use an observing ego to assess what behaviors mean, what relationships may exist to the analytic process. The narrative is thus merely a pleasurable exercise without a therapeutic goal or purpose. Another form of superficial communication does not involve libidinization; rather it is designed to camouflage something the patient does not want to discuss. This may be conscious or unconscious on the patient's part.

In dealing with the patient who "talks too much about nothing," it is often useful to point out that the patient's talking resembles a travelogue, a running narrative of external events, and thus keeps communication on a relatively superficial level. One might suggest that it is easier to engage in such reporting than to be truly introspective and get in touch with underlying thoughts and feelings, and that, in fact, the travelogue may be a form of defense.

Approaching the patient who libidinizes communication, the unconscious motive must first be understood. For example, is he relating material to be seductive, sexually provocative or exhibitionistic? Here, specific awareness of the countertransference feelings is essential in understanding the patient and prompt interpretations are indicated.

With the patient who libidinizes communication in the sense of engaging in narcissistic reverie concerning the events of his life, it is the therapist's responsibility to point out the nonproductive nature of such a gratification. He might say, for example, "This is very interesting but it does not help us understand your current conflicts and problems."

In dealing with the patient who engages in superficial narrative in order to camouflage conflicts, it is necessary to clarify for such a patient the defense involved. It often helps to relate a vignette such as the one about the school kids who devise a special maneuver when threatened with an exam: The brighter students organize and plot to ask the teacher as many questions as possible in order to monopolize the time so the exam cannot be given. Very often, patients camouflage in order to avoid a conflict-ridden issue.

Some patients—and even some therapists—believe simple catharsis, "blowing off steam," "getting things off one's chest," is curative in itself. However, this is a misconception. *Ventilation is not enough.* We must expect from a patient that one part of the self observe another part, i.e., that the objective or observing ego look at the preconscious and unconscious processes and report on them. The patient may get in touch with primary process material via free associations, fantasies, "daydreams," hypnogogic phenomenon and various stages of dreaming. At the same time the patient reports on this material, the self-observing function of the ego must also relate or connect the manifest thoughts to past apperceptions as insights. Again, this process involves some preconscious, unguided thinking (free association), some conscious awareness of the preconscious thoughts and the ability to see this primary process material in a new light—a new configuration—as part of a new Gestalt: This experience we call insight. A patient may, for instance, speak of anger against an employer, tell a dream of rage against a monster, relate this dream to rage against father and then, becoming aware of the sequence of thoughts and feelings, relate the dream to rage at the employer the day before, as well as to rage against the father in childhood. He thus becomes aware of the fact that part of his anger at his boss derives from the apperceptive distortion of the employer by the image of the father, i.e., that much of the anger was derived from much earlier feelings toward father.

In a well functioning analytic patient, the analytic process involves an oscillation between a *state of mind where conscious control over thoughts and feeling is relinquished* (a state in which free association can take place and preconscious and/or unconscious material is allowed to emerge, i.e., adaptive regression in the service of the ego, and *a state of mind where a fully conscious, observing ego takes an objective look at the unconscious interrelations.*

COMING LATE

Some patients come late to the therapeutic session habitually, or at least consistently during certain periods, as a form of acting-out. Other patients come late sporadically, engaging in unconsciously programmed behavior precipitated by certain sets of circumstances, also a form of acting-out. However, the obsessive-compulsive who is so overinvolved in preparing for the session that he comes in late is *not* acting out, strictly speaking. Such lateness does not have the quality of symptomatic acting-out, but is a part of the general lifestyle endemic to the obsessive character structure. Similarly, squeezing in too many activities before the appointment in a "desire to get the most out of time" is not necessarily acting-out. Lateness is closer to acting-out when it is a form of obstinacy: "Damned if I'm going to be on time!" This is acting-out as a form of revolt, typical of adolescence. The idea of a schedule is seen as an authoritarian symbol; the appointment time is often anthropomorphized as the authority. Coming late becomes a form of acting-out when, in the patient who has habitually come on time, the content of the analysis causes him to arrive late more or less in direct response to the conflictual material. For example, if in the analysis fears of death are aroused and lateness begins, it may be that time and the passage of time are equated with increasing closeness to death and, thus, coming late is a defense against the fear of dying. These differences in the meaning of the same manifest behavior, i.e., tardiness, *must* be clearly established if interpretations are to be at all valuable and lead to a cessation of the acting-out.

In dealing with lateness, the analyst must first ask himself what the patient is trying to express by his lateness. He will be able to find some clues by examining the countertransference feeling that the patient's lateness arouses in him: anger, anxiety, specific fantasies. The analyst's reaction is very likely related to the patient's own conflicts. Countertransference analysis in these cases can be an important adjunct tool for understanding the patient's unconscious motivation. The single most important therapeutic intervention for dealing with this behavior is interpretation of the specific unconscious meaning of the lateness.

NOT PAYING

If failure to pay the bill occurs as an isolated or rare episode rather than as a continuous pattern, it is especially likely to be a form of acting out a specific statement with an unconscious message—for example, "I want you to treat me for love rather than for money." Other motives may include the withholding of money much the way feces were withheld as a way of punishing mother or because of fear of a feeling of loss or of losing too much, producing a need to hold on for dear life. One can easily observe in many children a sense of distress or anxiety produced by seeing their feces flushed away. The feces are considered part of their body, part of themselves, and thus they feel a disturbing sense of loss. By the same token, some adults hate to part with money because they feel a part of them goes with it. Again interpretation of the unconscious motive for not paying is the key intervention. This should take a high priority since indebtedness to the therapist may lead to accumulated tension, which may well culminate in breaking off the therapeutic relationship. Owing money generates ill feelings. Gratitude is hard to bear, and often creates feelings of guilt and resentment in one who owes.

Financially and emotionally, few analysts can long afford the patient who, for whatever reason, does not pay the bills. Relatively few patients are responsible for the analyst's total income. Therefore, if one patient does not pay the analyst will feel this burden quite heavily. This differs from the situation with other caregiving professionals, such as general practitioners, who do not invest nearly as much time with each individual patient, and who can see many patients (as opposed to only one) during each office hour. The analyst's financial compensation does not approach that of other medical specialists.

It is important that the analyst examine the patient's financial basis on intake. He can help the patient assess the monetary aspect of the analytic arrangement, so that the ongoing analysis will not be disturbed by this factor. However, the analyst who uses a sliding scale should not necessarily set the fee during the first session. The patient may have more resources than he himself is aware of or, in some instances, than the analyst is aware of. In other cases, the patient unrealistically overestimates his financial ability. This may not become apparent during the initial interview. The analyst should establish a clear picture of the patient's financial situation over a period of time.

With the exception of very particular circumstances which have to be specifically arranged, it is not wise to permit a patient to default on payments for an extended period of time. Where reality situations such as divorce, loss of job, or other financial reversals cut back the patient's resources, the patient and therapist may negotiate payment and arrive at mutually agreeable adjustments and arrangements.

ACTING IN THE TRANSFERENCE

This term, coined by Anna Freud (1968) originally, is not very frequently used and has remained, in essence, confusing. I would like to use it in distinction to "transference resistance," and employ it to replace the term "erotization of the transference," since this latter term is too narrow and refers only to such problems as the patient's insisting that the analyst is primarily a love object, and not primarily an analyst. The term "erotization" of the transference is too restricted since often feelings other than sexual ones come into play and involve a loss of perspective on the part of the patient, i.e., they are not recognized as *transference* feelings but rather perceived as reality. For example, often hostile, paranoid, deprecatory and other traits and sentiments are ascribed to the analyst with the loss of the "as if" proposition. The patient is convinced that he perceives the therapist's character correctly and does not allow for his own apperceptive distortions as part of the transference.

A transference neurosis can be utilized provided the patient possesses enough of a healthy ego to realize, at least intermittently, that he is ascribing feelings about other significant figures from his childhood and other situations to the analyst, and that these feelings have an "as if" quality—he feels "as if" he were in love, "as if" he were angry, "as if" he were fearful. He maintains a necessary doubt regarding the *reality* of his feelings. This is achieved with the help of the reality testing function of his ego. It is essential that this "as if" attitude be maintained. If it is not, as when the reality testing function is impaired and the patient "loses distance," believing that, indeed, it is the *person* of the analyst whom he adores, hates, fears, etc., serious problems result.

To repeat, then, I believe that the term "acting in the transference" could usefully be used to mean a transference relationship that has lost its "as if" character, has lost its distance. This stands in distinction to "acting out in the transference" where feelings felt for the analyst are being ascribed to others outside the therapeutic situation, e.g., the case where a patient falls in love with some other analyst in his or her acquaintaince or some person resembling the analyst in any one of a variety of features, size, look, ethnic background. Acting out in the transference thus involves a transference of the feelings felt for the analyst and generated in the course of the analysis from childhood memories, dreams, etc. to people on the outside of the analytic situation.

In addition, acting out in the transference to some extent involves the patient's expressing feelings and perhaps directing some actions toward the analyst which are meant for and stem from feelings towards historical figures, or even contemporary figures outside therapy. That is, acting out in the transference involves a two-way distortion: 1) distorting external relationships by displacing onto others feelings for the analyst, and 2) distorting feelings toward the analyst by having them colored by feelings for and about historical and possibly contemporary figures.

However, in spite of this two-way distortion, the patient who is acting out in the transference is nevertheless able to maintain some distance and the "as if" nature of the therapeutic relationship, in distinction to acting in the transference where the "as if" quality and distance are lost.

By definition, acting in the transference involves more seriously ill people, whether they are acting in an eroticized transference, a paranoid one or some other variety. It is, in essence, a breakdown of the therapeutic alliance, which states that the healthy part of the ego continues to maintain enough distance to permit the observing function to operate and to be allied with the analyst, who is perceived clearly as a therapist.

Acting in the transference is a serious problem which may, at the very least, lead to interruption of the therapy, because the patient either feels unloved in his or her real quest or becomes unduly suspicious of the therapist and possibly even dangerous in his paranoia. The countertransference problems are also serious under such circumstances and probably occur most often when a therapist loses distance himself and feels sufficiently flattered by and involved with the patient to be available for a real relationship. This may involve an inappropriate love relationship on the part of both therapist and patient.

Specific measures for dealing with acting in the transference involve vigorous reality testing, invoking of the therapeutic alliance, and interpretations which clarify the desire for acting in the transference.

If the acting in is especially severe, it has long been my practice to refer such a patient temporarily to an *auxiliary therapist,* whose main task is to analyze the pathological transference relationship. Probably in both the case of an eroticized transference and one of paranoid acting in the transference, a therapist of the *sex opposite to the primary therapist* serves best as the auxiliary therapist. Under these new circumstances, it is easier to handle the transference problems involving the primary therapist. Such instances should be considered matters of emergency intervention, which must be handled skillfully, with clear-cut areas of intervention and methods of intervention. This same specificity of intervention is, of course, that which is indicated in all emergency psychotherapy. Referring to an auxiliary therapist obviously is not the intervention indicated if the specific function of acting-out is precisely that of interrupting therapy. Such an intervention would then be feeding into the patient's acting-out.

NEGATIVE THERAPEUTIC RESPONSE

A negative therapeutic response occurs when the patient has every reason to respond with an improvement in terms of the analytic process, but instead there is a sharp worsening of his situation. The analyst is pleased with successful interpretations and with the progress of the analysis, but the patient, rather than experiencing relief, will respond with an anxiety attack, a depression, or some other indication of a negative therapeutic response. Typically, this happens in the patient with a severe superego, for whom all success is equated with the attainment of the forbidden oedipal object. Under these regrettable circumstances, even the attainment of better health and greater happiness due to therapeutic success will fall under the heading of forbidden attainment and, under the impact of the superego, make the patient feel worse instead of better.

The negative therapeutic response is a symptomatic reaction; the patient feels guilty about feeling better.

Negative therapeutic response belongs under the concept of acting-out, as it involves *a very definite dynamic configuration and programmed sequence of behavior.* One such dynamic configuration would be the success neurosis which would lead a person to repeated and programmed failures. This dynamic constellation may also lead to a negative transference on a superficial basis. The patient will question the wisdom of the treatment; he will perceive himself getting worse instead of better. The patient's negative feelings for one of his parents are frequently projected onto the therapist, feelings which are actually a defense against some of the positive feelings in the oedipal setting. Therefore, the analyst will have to work through the superego aspects of the forbidden oedipal strivings, as well as the additional transference problems particular to the situation.

Alternatively, sometimes the patient's experience of feeling worse may be due to his not wanting the analyst to have the satisfaction that he is getting better. At other times the patient is afraid that the analyst will lose interest in him and perhaps abandon him now that he is getting better.

It is extremely difficult to work with a negative therapeutic response. Naturally, one tries to interpret repeatedly any aspects of the basic situation which appear, namely, the equation of any success, including any therapeutic success, with forbidden oedipal attainment, and the moral masochism that compels the patient to make himself become worse again. Heavy emphasis should be based on the contemporary analytic situation. Undoubtedly some aggressive impulses are directed toward the analyst as a parental identification figure. A measure of spite enters in, a feeling of "Damned if I'll let you win over me." This is a fighting off of passivity. Any improvement is seen as a victory for the analyst and as a defeat of the patient.

Other features that often play a role have to do with the secondary gain in remaining ill. For instance, a patient with a success neurosis, who habitually became worse every Christmas season when his business was doing particularly well, had a further realistic complication, namely the time had come for him to take over the family business and, however pleasantly, force his father out of the controlling position. Reality then added a good deal to the basic, unconscious oedipal guilt. In addition, he suffered from an agoraphobia, which, as usual, was related to an ambivalent attachment and some symbiosis with the mother. Assuming his new role as head of the company would also force mother out of her participation in the business. She had been the power behind father's throne and in addition had played a controlling role vis-à-vis the patient's own work. The patient was also threatened, therefore, of being deprived of her nurturance. It thus turned out that, in addition to oedipal guilt toward father, some of the negative therapeutic response was related to his mother. When this patient had particular reason to feel well, and had already responded to therapy with a complete lack of symptoms for several months, he not only became depressed again in terms of his success neurosis, but had a return of phobic symptoms and hypochondriacal reactions, to a considerable extent as the wish to remain dependent on mother, along with the usual fears of his aggression towards mother and the wish to separate himself from her.

The fact is that a negative therapeutic reaction appears like a ship tied to the dock by many strands of rope. One frequently must go on looking for other yet hidden ties that keep the boat, the patient, from being able to float freely. Above all, this holds true for the many facets of the transference relationship.

THREATENING TO BREAK OFF

When a patient threatens to break off treatment, some of the most general principles for dealing with acting-out are the most useful. Anticipate the threatened acting-out. When you see it coming, communicate your perceptions to the patient. Even in the anamnesis, there may be evidence that acting-out in the form of breaking-off is a possibility. If so, it would be appropriate even at the initial interview to say, "You know, with your personality structure, it is very likely you might want to break off therapy prematurely. Look at your pattern of behavior with many other people in your life where you have broken things off. It is therefore only reasonable to assume that at some point you might get mad at me, feel this is too much, or too threatening, and want to call it quits."

If, in fact, the patient does threaten to leave therapy prematurely, anticipate the consequences. "Let's look at what will happen if you break off now. You will only be reinforcing the same old pattern which will not be very constructive." Bargain for a delay. The patient cannot be held in analysis. However, if the idea of the patient's giving a week's advance notice before leaving therapy has been established at the time of the initial contract, he can be reminded that he has at least that period of time to discuss whatever is on his mind and to think through any major decisions, including breaking off treatment. If the patient agrees to use this time, the analyst then has a chance to analyze and interpret the primary conflict leading to the patient's need to act out. Furthermore, when the feeling of *urgency* to flee cannot find an immediate outlet, much of the intensity of this desire will disappear. Finally, if the transference situation has become unbearable and arouses so much anxiety that a break-off of therapy is imminent, the analyst can change the patient's position from the couch to the chair. This places less pressure on the unconscious and structures the situation. In addition, the analyst can also talk to the patient in a more educational way, reviewing the gains made and making some intellectual interpretations. These techniques will dilute the otherwise highly charged situation and help control the amount of anxiety-arousing material.

With the threat to break off, the patient might be saying, "You are controlling me; you are no good; you don't help me; you don't love me enough. Therefore I don't love you." It may also be a sadistic aggressive statement. "I'll show you; you need my money; you'll be sorry not to have me." In the life history, it is likely that someone was sadistic and rejecting towards the patient, and that he sometimes puts himself in the masochistic position. However, sometimes one is dealing with transference feelings that are simply unbearable to the patient and it is impossible to prevent the patient from breaking off therapy. Some patients may have to leave therapy for a time, to return later on. Each episode of treatment takes them so far; then they are compelled to flee. A patient with homosexual anxiety toward his therapist had a dream about being chased by a chimpanzee who resembled the therapist. No amount of interpretation could make staying in treatment bearable for the patient, nor would he take any medication because this also constituted a form of control over him, symbolizing sexual submission which he could not tolerate. Other patients seem to have a low frustration tolerance, as well as a low anxiety tolerance. A very creative man who worked very hard in the analytic situation would "come upon" some career opportunity that he would magically endow with the power to answer all his problems, and thus be tempted again and again to leave therapy. He left and returned to therapy several times when the magic collapsed.

FLIGHT INTO HEALTH

Flight into health is Freud's term for a patient who suddenly becomes much better and purports to be cured. This declaration usually does not have much basis in fact. It often occurs in response to some painful recollection, a memory which may occur spontaneously, or to some premature, painful uncovering. As discussed by Glover (1955), the primary defense mechanism behind most acting-out is *denial*. With the denial goes the false sense of well-being that is typical for denial, most outstandingly in hypomanic and manic patients. The other characteristic of this form of acting-out is its *urgency*. The patient insists that he is cured and that he must leave analysis immediately. In dealing with flight into health, the analyst should form a clear picture of exactly at what point in time the flight began. For instance, three sessions previously the patient had a painful recollection, the analyst made an interpretation and since that time the patient has not really talked about anything appropriate to this situation. The patient has engaged in what Lewin (1950) described as *centrifugal-type associations*—associations which deal with disturbing material by denying the central focus. Everything the patient discusses seems to lead away from this center. If the analyst listens carefully, he can usually discern what the patient is denying, from what issue he is fleeing. An interpretation regarding the motivation for the patient's escape or flight into health will often instantaneously produce a depression, but it is nevertheless an important and appropriate intervention, since the goal is to help the patient forestall acting-out and remain in therapy where his problems can be treated.

If the analyst is aware of the patient's denial, he can bring him back to the center by reviewing the material covered in previous sessions that the patient is avoiding, interpreting the denial of the painful situation or conflict, and engaging in concurrent reality testing. One patient felt he could stop therapy because he felt as if he were "more than two-thirds better." It was suggested that if he drove off a bridge two-thirds of the way across he would not be safely on the other side. Aside from general measures such as interpretation and reality testing, when dealing with a flight into health, above all, the analyst should work for a delay in the acting-out.

REFERENCES

FREUD, A. Acting out. *International Journal of Psycho-Analysis,* 49, 165-70, 1963.
GLOVER, E. *The Technique of Psychoanalysis.* New York: International Universities Press, 1955.
LEWIN, B. D. *The Psychoanalysis of Elation.* New York: W. W. Norton, 1950.

12. General Transference Problems

Concepts of transference in the literature vary a great deal. Definitions of transference phenomena are difficult; however, it is necessary to identify and clearly conceptualize the processes which may at times lead to dire situations in the "transference relationship."

The analytic/therapeutic situation itself makes great demands on the patient. For some decades, because it is in so many ways a difficult task, only relatively intact people were chosen for classical analysis. The analyst demands an "as if" relationship. He expects a close relationship to be established, but that he not be mistaken for a *real* object. It is part of the therapeutic contract that he be seen as an extrapolated object. For instance, the patient will get angry with the analyst, but his ego must be healthy enough to reality test and realize that his anger is probably not appropriate and does not have to do with the person of the analyst, but with apperceptive distortions based on his past experiences. The patient must be willing to look at his behavior and explore his feelings, while at the same time experiencing, within limits, real anger. At times the patient must permit regressions to take place in order that the ego may engage in free association, "a willing suspension of disbelief" or critical faculties, while at other times he must be able to engage in extensive reality testing. This is a very difficult task.

130

In analysis or therapy, the patient does not get the usual feedback that he would receive in any social situation. In the latter, his apperceptive distortions, positive or negative, are often corrected rather promptly by the reactions of others. Much exogenous reality testing is a consensual validation via other people to an extent which the analytic therapist does not provide. However, the advantage of the therapist remaining "anonymous" and observing "therapeutic neutrality" is that it facilitates apperceptive distortions and thus examination on the part of the patient in the analytic situation.

Some have said that everything that happens in analysis is a transference phenomenon. This definition is too broad and also misleading. The therapeutic alliance is not to be mistaken for a transference relationship; various foibles of the analyst and countertransference phenomena may be accurately observed by the patient. The broad definition that Greenson (1967) offers is one where transference is seen as a repetition of some parts of the past which are inappropriate to the present. This is hardly different from the general phenomena of apperceptive distortion or projection which occurs in all of us in relation to many people to a greater or lesser degree.

More narrowly, two concepts that most analysts differentiate are transference reactions and transference neuroses. The transference reaction occurs in all types of relationships. It is, in essence, a "transferral" or carrying over of sentiments, drives, and conflicts experienced in the past to current situations and people. In this sense one may have transference reactions to employers or teachers or many others, including the therapist. The transference reaction to the therapist is frequently more marked than most others, although not necessarily. For instance, the relationship of some women to their obstetricians can be very intense. The interactions with both the therapist and the physician are characterized by unique intimacy and dependence, and are thus susceptible to greater distortion.

The transference neurosis proper occurs only in classical analysis. Via the analysis of defenses, the analyst creates a planned, methodical regression, to the point where a childhood neurosis is revived in the analytic relationship. This transference neurosis serves as a laboratory model on which the analyst can work. In fact, many past dynamic problems which have not been specifically discussed in analysis appear and are resolved automatically as a consequence of the analysis of the transference problems. Resolution of the conflicts manifested in this laboratory-reproduced mini-micro-model of earlier relationships and occurrences takes place through transfer of training and other learning processes.

The transference neurosis will wax and wane. The patient who is increasingly anxious due to the analysis of defenses is experiencing an intensification of the transference neurosis, an increase in his apperceptive distortions. This is worked through in the process of analysis, usually with much less *residual* apperceptive distortion. In this process the analyst must deal with many facets and phases of the transference neurosis. As one dynamic problem is worked through, another relating to a different phase of development may be activated. There will be many different types of transference neuroses and reactions produced in the analytic process, with repeated waxing, working-through, and waning.

For example, if a patient becomes inappropriately angry in response to some frustration and the analyst not only does not respond but also analyzes the patient's response to the frustration, the result will be a rolling back of the defenses in a manner which is demonstrated in an oversimplified way by Mowrer (1940) in an experiment on regression: He placed some white rats on a grill which, under some circumstances, gave them an electric shock which could be aborted when the rats learned to push a lever with their noses. When the rules were changed and pushing the lever did not turn off the shock but standing on their hind legs did, they learned the second response as well. But when the rules were changed again and standing on their hind legs did not help, all returned to the earlier learned behavior and pushed the lever with their noses. Similarly, *when defenses become inoperative, the patient is likely to return to earlier modes of adaptation.* The patient who responds to frustration with anger may next suck his thumb as a regressive form of response.

The main difficulties arising out of these transference manifestations develop because the dissociative role in this relationship is a very difficult one. *Resistance to transference* and *transference re-*

sistance are the two major problems to be anticipated because of this difficulty.

Transference resistance occurs when the patient wants to relate to the analyst as a real object and does not want to engage in the therapeutic alliance and follow the therapeutic contract. He will not willingly engage in the necessary dissociation, where one part of the self reports on inner feelings and fantasies no matter how irrational and the other part observes this process as objectively as possible and intermittently exercises judgment. When the patient fails to see the analyst as a transitional object, something can occur similar to a phenomenon Freud first encountered—his patients "fell in love with him." It is to his credit that he did not let this alarm him to the point of breaking off treatment for fear of causing a scandal, but realized that the patient's feelings for him were a repetition of earlier relationships. Thus the concept of transference phenomena was born. If the patient insists that the analyst is the one person he or she really loves, if the patient's only goal is to promote a love relationship with the analyst, analysis will be impossible.

Resistance to the transference occurs if the patient is unwilling and/or unable to engage in the willing suspension of his critical faculties and enter into an "as if" relationship. He does not free associate, he talks correctly, and he does not develop any feeling for the analyst, even the ordinary human feelings that would come from sharing very intimate problems with another person, day after day. He resists the development of any transference feelings or reactions, and most importantly, the transference neurosis. The superficial aspects of the working alliance may be adhered to well enough—he presents material for the analysis, comes on time, etc., but the analysis will not progress. The particular resistance to the therapeutic relationship and the whole idea of therapy will have to be analyzed first.

ANAMNESIS AND ASSESSMENT

A careful history—anamnesis and assessment—will reveal certain types of patients who are likely to develop more or less specific types of transference problems.

Disruptive transference phenomena can occur especially if the patient has been in treatment previously. The transference relationship to the other analyst should be analyzed, as well as pertinent specific information about the circumstances of treatment. Transference manifestations that pertain still to the previous therapist will undoubtedly appear and need to be understood as such.

The hysterical patient will come with many physical complaints and demand a supportive relationship with the analyst. The transference affect of the hysterical patient is very fluid and is usually characterized by an excess of affect, either overvaluating the therapist or negatively undervaluating.

The obsessive patient most frequently manifests resistance to the transference. He is often afraid to let stray emotions and irrational feelings emerge. Adaptive regression in the service of the ego is difficult and threatening in that it may imply loss of control. This resistance to transference usually takes the form of concrete thinking, reaction formations, and, above all, projections of his superego onto the analyst. The patient believes the analyst thinks poorly of him and is judging him unfavorably. He is, therefore, reluctant to talk for fear of underscoring the feeling that he is a terrible person. Interpretations are frequently reacted to as criticism.

The phobic patient will display an *ambivalent* relationship to the analyst, in accordance with the basic dynamics of phobias towards a significant early figure, usually a mother. Phobic patients earlier defended against their ambivalence by developing a very dependent relationship to her, and this is relived in the transference situation. Since, under such circumstances, the analyst is often used as a counterphobic device, his presence is used for protection against evil happenings. As long as the analyst is available, the patient will feel secure. As soon as the analyst is unavailable, the situation with the patient becomes much worse, as in weekend and vacation neuroses.

Borderline patients (and some obsessive patients) will at times display little in the way of object relationship. Some regard the therapist as a machine. They come for a session, say their piece and wait for the therapist in turn to offer his. Then they leave, displaying little or no affective relationship to the therapist. On the other hand, some with poor self-boundaries display even more fluid and violent transient affect than the hysterical patient. Excessive distortions, insisting that the analyst sees the patient as stupid, that relating to the analyst leads to the patient's weakening and the analyst's controlling of him are salient features.

Depressed psychotic patients will usually develop a marked dependence on the therapist. Through long stretches of even a rather classical analysis, depressed patients who are unable to relate should be actively supported until they are able to analyze again.

Psychotic patients will have difficult and stormy transference problems, due to psychotic-level distortions of positive and negative kinds and the added potentiality of acting-out in that psychotic transference. Anticipation of problems is especially crucial in these cases, because of the inherent dangers in any break with reality.

MANAGEMENT

With fairly disturbed people, the analyst will have to work with the patient's concrete concerns and be supportive, discussing all sorts of reality aspects. Some patients will need this as part of every session for a long time. When the patient feels the therapist has shown enough interest in him and he has made sufficient progress, the therapist can then slowly proceed to other aspects of analysis and begin to interpret each time resistance to transference arises. It may be pointed out, for example, that the resistance is an expression of the wish to be taken care of.

It may sometimes be a good strategy to use an *auxiliary therapist* whose primary job is to analyze the transference with the initial therapist. This is an important emergency measure. It introduces a measure of reality testing for the patient and dilutes the transference reaction to the primary therapist. This tactic may sometimes be necessary when the patient shows resistance to transference and resistance to the therapeutic alliance.

Sometimes transference problems cause a patient to seek a consultation with another analyst or therapist. Every patient has a right to seek a consultation and every therapist has a right to see such a patient. If the patient is found to be obviously acting out and the original therapist appears competent, the consultant's task is easy.

Technical, emotional and ethical difficulties arise if the analyst consulted decides that the patient has good reason for not wanting to continue with his present therapist. The consulting analyst can feel more impartial if he informs the patient initially that he will serve as consultant, but will not be able to take him into treatment. It is easiest for the patient and the therapists if the probability of a self-serving critical attitude is minimized. Under these conditions, the therapist who is acting as consultant finds it easier to carry out his proper function, i.e., to be impartial and not to hesitate to tell the patient if he feels the therapy in which he is engaged is not productive and a change of therapists is indicated. We owe this to patients.

If the patient wants to see another therapist without his present therapist's knowledge, the rights of the patient come before professional courtesy. The patient should be seen in consultation and given an objective appraisal. Sometimes patients' concern and questions about the therapy they have been undergoing are entirely justified and should be supported.

Glover (1955) has suggested that failure to benefit from analysis may be related to another specific kind of transference resistance: the patient's substitution of the analyst's benign and nonjudgmental presence for his own very punitive superego. The patient would rather keep his symptoms than let go of the comfortable analytic situation and avoid making the step toward internalization and restructuring.

Some patients "resist" by being involved in one crisis after another. By creating constant upheavals in reality, the patient attempts to avoid the internal problems and the exploration of the unconscious.

For example, a man who presented with a marked preoccupation with neurological difficulties following three major episodes of illness had a great deal of difficulty with insight, the therapeutic alliance and resistance to the transference. Most sessions began with a list of serious, sometimes physical, complaints. He read about various neurological disorders. The way he described his symptoms was, however, inconsistent. Interpretation of this resistance was mixed with a supportive approach in recognition of his great need for reassurance. He was urged, despite the inconsistency, to seek alternative neurological consultation and even provided with the names of a few reputable physicians. Listening to and responding to the essential message, "I'm sick. I need help," satisfied to some degree the patient's need along these lines and permitted the analysis to proceed a little further with interpretive work in each session. He eventually revealed a migratory castration anxiety reaching back to his childhood, when he had spent much time in bed with his mother.

Not all patients can analyze well from the start. In fact, selecting only patients who can do so from the beginning will soon lead to an empty practice and a cripplingly narrow repertoire of clinical skills.

REFERENCES

GLOVER, E. *The Technique of Psychoanalysis.* New York: International Universities Press, 1955.

GREENSON, R. R. *The Technique and Practice of Psychoanalysis,* Vol. 1. New York: International Universities Press, 1967.

MOWRER, O. H. An experimental analogue of "regression" with incidental observations on "reaction-formation." *Journal of Abnormal and Social Psychology,* Vol. 135, 1940, 56-87.

13. General Countertransference Problems

Lay people often ask of a psychiatrist, referring to our patients, "How can you stand such people?" Indeed, one's patients may present aspects of themselves that are unpleasant or patently disturbed. An attitude of compassion for the human condition is most helpful. A Viennese proverb notes, "Human, human are we all." And Terentius, "I am human. Nothing human is strange to me." Everyone reflects only slightly more or less unique distortions of the human experience, and sincere compassion for the pain of our patients need not be difficult to find. The pain is especially acute when the patient himself recognizes that his behavior is less than enchanting and raises the question of the analyst's liking him. Boyer and Giovacchini (1967) formulate it this way: The analyst does not have to like *all* of the patient, everything about him. It is enough that he like him as a person. The aspects that he does not like need not interfere with the analysis. In fact, these aspects may represent pathological parts of the personality, the treatment of which are thus proper goals of analysis.

To be distinguished from our feelings and reactions to our patients based on their *actual* personalities, countertransference is defined as the *apperceptive distortions that occur in the therapist*

138

in relation to the patient. In the therapeutic relationship, a great many affective processes occur in both doctor and patient. The patient may be identified with figures from the therapist's past. Or the patient may arouse certain conflicts and emotions from the therapist's past or present which, in their irrationality, will hinder the analyst in his treatment of the patient unless he explores and analyzes these countertransference feelings. Such feelings can and do lead to seriously disruptive phenomenon and must be *continually* monitored and analyzed.

ANAMNESIS AND ASSESSMENT

When "dislike" does enter the analysis, it is important—in fact, essential, to understand its nature. It may appear as a defense against anxiety of many different kinds, such as homosexual or hetero-sexual anxiety problems of aggression—in fact, the whole spectrum of struggles to which man is heir. The patient may represent an unacceptable part of the analyst—and most of us are unable to tolerate in others what disturbs us most about ourselves.

Some patients produce realistic anxiety in the analyst because they perpetrate or are involved in threatening and dangerous situations and activities. If the patient is suicidal, it is only reasonable to be highly concerned. Extremely disturbed people are especially likely to create very difficult situations in and out of the therapy, the stresses of which are sure to produce countertransference problems for the analyst. While individual political persuasions and business activities are usually of little concern in analysis, people involved in sociopathic, illegal, ideologically corrupt or otherwise dangerous situations introduce a variable which can only interfere with the analysis. The immediate dangers and moral dilemmas for both the patient and the analyst are simply too discomforting for analytic work to proceed simultaneously. It is an either/or situation.

Anger in the therapist toward his patient may be an understand-able and realistic reaction to part of the patient's personality which is problematic and should be analyzed. However, it may also be, in some very variable measure, the analyst's response to the feeling that his omnipotence is being threatened by the patient's provocative, inappropriate, or grossly disturbed behaviors. Certainly, we like our patients to get better, and rescue fantasies are likely to be somewhat active in us, whatever the stage of our career. Thus, if the patient does not oblige by improving, the analyst may react with anger. He may feel, inappropriately, that the patient is ungrateful. The analyst must understand these wishes and learn to live with the limitations of his profession, which so often produces less than miraculous and inspiring cures.

The therapist may, at times, find a patient boring. This can be very disruptive to the therapeutic process. Patients will differ in terms of how interesting they are to us, and occasionally some are less than fascinating. But here again, while the analysis of the countertransference may reveal something about the patient (most obviously resistance), boredom is often an indicator of anxiety on the part of the analyst. In the extreme, the analyst may find himself falling asleep!

At the other end of the spectrum is the countertransference problem so often in the public eye—falling in love with one's patient. If the analyst finds that he has sexual feelings toward his patient and the patient is not doing specific things to provoke these emotions, the analyst must then analyze his own feelings, fantasies, and needs. A love relationship with one's patient is usually not successful. The analyst can function best at an optimum distance where he is compassionately involved but at the same time not so close that he loses judgment. Falling in love with a patient is invariably due to a countertransference phenomenon that involves a disturbance in judgment. The analyst is probably falling in love with his own handiwork, with his own skill as reflected in the patient's condition. The more narcissistic analyst will have to be especially careful of this "Pygmalion" syndrome.

Searles (1965) feels, especially with psychotic patients, that as part of the natural process of treatment, the analyst will have erotic feelings toward his patient, and that it will in some way retard treatment if he blocks those feelings. In part, Searles can work well with schizophrenic patients because of his own empathic personality. This is his own way of experiencing and empathizing with patients, but it is not a method with which most analysts would be comfortable. There are varying degrees of being involved with one's patients and one does not have to be emotionally disturbed or highly susceptible to have erotic feelings toward them, but how intense should the analyst allow the feelings to become? Searles feels that he should share his feelings with his patients, that he should tell them about his life and troubles. But where do you draw the line? It is only human to have erotic feelings toward some patients at some times, but they must be kept within certain bounds to permit the analyst to maintain his objectivity and perspective. While some therapists share their problems with their patients, and under some circumstances it may be useful to relate something about yourself to a patient, with a specific therapeutic purpose in mind—for example, fostering identification, serving as an introject, etc.—the patient comes to the analyst for treatment, not to be burdened with someone else's problems. Searles treats the analytic situation as a two-way street, but excessively so, for the good of the patient.

Certainly some analysts are much too stiff with their patients and never allow themselves to appear human. In fact, as a clearly conceptualized strategy, it is sometimes useful to talk to a patient about one's own foibles or peculiarities, sharing part of the human condition in order to help the patient deal with some of his own unrealistic fears or expectations, difficulties and imperfections. This is not routine, however, and must be carefully thought out and continually monitored for any taint of countertransference.

MANAGEMENT

The answer to the problem of countertransference and the threat it poses in terms of disruption of the analytic process is a *continual self-monitoring* and the use of the *countertransference feelings as an added way of understanding the patient's behavior*. The feelings the patient produces in the analyst can be an important indication of what is going on in the patient. For example, if the patient produces in us a feeling of frustration and anger, this may well be what the patient feels. The patient may consciously or unconsciously wish to make others feel what he has been made to suffer. A variation of an old adage describes this human tendency: Do unto others what you feel has been done to you. However, staying in touch with one's own countertransference feelings, recognizing the factors and circumstances which produce them, and finding reasonable and meaningful strategies and tactics for dealing with them are difficult tasks and therefore require extra vigilance and effort.

Through this process of identifying the source of countertransference feelings, the therapist is put in touch with the reality of the patient's situation. For example, if the patient arouses anxiety in us because of certain personal and/or environmental handicaps inherent to his condition, recognizing and coming to terms with these real limitations are necessary on the analyst's part if he is to continue to be helpful. On occasion, in the face of impossible, realistic circumstances, one must deal with the fact that psychotherapy is severely limited, if not unworkable. A triage, of sorts, is necessary—reaching decisions, as difficult as they may be, that there are some people well enough not to need immediate care and others so disturbed that it isn't likely that anyone can do much. Saving our energies for those in between who are likely to profit from treatment may be the best course at the present state of the art.

Only if the patient and the therapist are relatively free from realistic anxiety can they enter into the more complex process of discovering the psychological origins of specific problems. Whatever is most urgent will have to be dealt with first. For instance, the daughter of a criminal family may find it difficult to talk about that family's activities and, of course, hearing of secret unlawful activities may compromise and jeopardize the safety of the therapist. More commonly, a person in the throes of a tumultuous divorce may be able to talk about little aside from that painful reality. You may have to settle for doing a brief, focal, emergency psychotherapy.

Larger ethical issues, personal conflicts about issues such as abortion, third-party payers and patient rights, or political activism may all interfere with the therapist's judgment. The therapist may try to alter the circumstances by having the patient declare a moratorium on dangerous or provocative behaviors. But if the therapist is too anxious, too emotionally involved, there should be no equivocation. Stop the therapy and, if the problem or behavior is not totally ego-syntonic, the patient reasonably motivated, and some alternative adaptation conceivable, refer the patient to another therapist. One may use the auxiliary therapist as a consultant to seek an alternative treatment plan where the initial therapist's perspective has been compromised, but one ought also to be prepared to recognize immutable factors in the patient and/or therapist that yield insurmountable countertransference obstacles in the specific chemistry at hand. The therapist must then respectfully shake the patient's hand and wish him well with another therapist.

REFERENCES

BOYER, L. & GIOVACCHINI, P. *Psychoanalytic Treatment of Characterological and Schizophrenic Disorders.* New York: Science House, 1967.

SEARLES, H. *Collected Papers on Schizophrenia and Related Subjects.* New York: International Universities Press, 1965.

14. Stalemate

Of all the problems that can appear in analysis, stalemate, as Glover has called it (1955), is the most frequent. As the term suggests, stalemate means that things have gone stale, they don't move forward. A temporary stalemate is part of any learning process; the plateau is a widely recognized phenomenon. The same leveling off situation vis-à-vis insight and conflict resolution can, and often does, hold true for therapy or analysis.

A temporary lull or halt in the therapeutic progress may certainly be a matter of defense against depression, anxiety, etc. Such a deadlock can often be remedied promptly by the correct interpretation of the defense; however, when, after the seemingly appropriate interventions have been made, still no significant material is forthcoming, when you have reached not only the point of diminishing returns but of no returns, when, despite your various attempts at intervention, both you and the patient have a feeling of boredom, of not accomplishing anything—then you have reached a stalemate. Often, a stalemate is transient and will undergo spontaneous resolution depending on the clinical situation. However, if it persists, the patient will terminate under much less favorable circumstances than would be the case if the therapist made some active intervention, even including planned termination, with the possibility of resuming treatment sometime in the future. Appropriate measures will benefit the patient's current attitude toward the psychotherapeutic process and facilitate a return to treatment if and when the patient is willing and able to engage in further self-exploration and conflict resolution.

Viewing pyschoanalysis or psychotherapy as a process of learning by insight, conditioning, and identification, we must assume that *some* limits in terms of reversibility are inevitable. Other limitations may, however, be transient: Frequently, we must accept the premise that many patients will learn by "dispersal of training," rather than by one concentrated effort. Academic psychology generally thinks well of this type of learning. Such piecemeal learning can be compared to memorizing part of a poem today, part tomorrow, and so forth, rather than attempting to memorize the whole poem in one day. This theory of learning applied to the therapeutic process means that some patients may need a pause of six months or a year or even several years, during which time "silent learning" may take place, a time when they will have the opportunity to use what has been previously learned in treatment. During this period away from therapy it is also possible that a reality situation which contributed to the original stalemate (for example, a financial reversal) may improve, which then makes it possible to resume further therapy.

Of course, an attempt should be made to avoid stalemates in the first place. The basic proposition, after all, is that analysis is a *process* which begins with the therapeutic alliance and the therapeutic contract. It is the analyst's job to keep the process moving by maintaining a clear conceptualization of the patient's basic history and psychodynamics, as well as the propositions concerning psychology in general and the psychology of each patient in particular. The therapist must select those areas and methods of intervention in the specific sequence most likely to move the process toward a desirable goal, to make the patient more adaptive and happier. When the analyst does not perform his job the way it has just been defined, stalemate is likely to occur. Good technique involves the appropriate management of transference and countertransference manifestations and, in general, a resolution of the patient's main conflicts, along with a restructuring of his pathological internal structures and apperceptive distortions.

In summary, then, stalemate is a deadlocking of the analytic process, often due to a lack of clear conceptualization and adequate technique. When the analyst does not have a well defined notion of where to go and/or what to do, the analysis is impaired. This interference includes going off on tangents, failing to deal with resistances, focusing on side issues (introduced by the patient or by reality), and engaging in what Freud called a "wild analysis" or others might call "a wild goose chase." This unsystematic approach involves analyzing whatever material is presented, especially translating unconscious processes directly, instead of carefully selecting appropriate areas for interpretation and working-through. While analyzing primary process material, whatever it may be, is often tempting for the analyst, it may have nothing to do with the *central* problems that must eventually be dealt with. Pursuing side issues at the expense of focusing on the central problems at that time is simply poor technique.

ANAMNESIS AND ASSESSMENT

When something interferes with the flow of the analytic process, with conceptualizing and managing the transference and countertransference issues, and with the resolution of fundamental conflicts leading to internal restructuring, the manifestations of this stalemate may be many and varied. Reality factors and circumstances may play some role in creating a stalemate but internal factors and therapeutic technique are likely to make a more significant contribution. Internal factors introduced by the patient vary from general defenses against anxiety and depression to specific types of failures of the analytic process, for example, flight into health, negative therapeutic response, or transference resistance. The potential for failing to maximize the objectives of the therapeutic alliance and contract poses a constant temptation and threat for the less than rigorous and steadfast clinician. Ideally, adequate anamnesis and assessment, as defined in Chapter 2, is the preventive to stalemate, but it also helps to find the cure if the process is faltering.

MANAGEMENT

In a stalemate, the analyst must first review the history, the symptomatology, and the patient's present stage of analysis. He must ask himself: What has possibly been overlooked in terms of the common denominators and the resistances? Where are the conceptual hypotheses incorrect? Every therapist sometimes operates on a wrong hypothesis. The relationships between the material presented in the last session and the several preceding sessions must be examined within the overall framework of the patient's personality problems and life history. If the relationship is not evident, if the fit is not perfect, the analyst must realign his hypotheses. Some emerging themes and resistances to them, especially transference problems, may not have been recognized and, therefore, not analyzed.

Reviewing the dynamic situation, however, may not always help break a deadlock. The patient may have been well analyzed but an optimal result may not be possible due to the fact that some reality situation remains unresolved. For example, he or she may be in an ongoing outside relationship that interferes with treatment, such as a marriage based originally on a pathological object choice.

In one case, a patient who was originally suicidal, paranoid, and extremely constricted did very well in analysis with regard to all of these problems. Towards the end of the analysis, she was unable to choose between her handsome, well-to-do husband, who was pleasant in many ways but nevertheless narcissistic and sexually inadequate, and a devoted and adequate lover who, although interesting and interested in her, could not support her in the manner to which she had become accustomed. She had to choose, in this difficult reality situation, between her lover and a comfortable peer-approved marital situation, which also involved two children. Unlike Ingrid Bergman, this woman chose to remain with her husband. Follow-up showed that she was living a contented life, free of disturbing symptoms, but she had by no means reached the level of functioning in all spheres that she was likely to have achieved with the other man. On the other hand, I could not *absolutely* guarantee that, had she chosen the lover, she could have endured or been happy in a totally different socioeconomic setting. In this case I maintained neutrality because I had no choice to suggest.

In some instances, the analyst may attempt to change some of the field, affecting the "other players" or altering the reality situation so as to interfere with the stalemate. For example, a continued dependence on a parent may play a major role in creating a block to further growth and can be analyzed *ad nauseam*, but often, unless the reality situation is changed, nothing else can be done and there is no point in continuing the analysis. It behooves one then to encourage the patient to forego the advantages of financial dependence and/or the gratifications of psychological dependence in order to attain emotional freedom. This may mean encouraging a young man to leave a well-paying position in his family's or his wife's family's business, if such a position involves a double-bind.

To reiterate, with regard to reality situations, the practical limitations often limit the reversibility of psychopathology. If these outside limitations involve the patient's relationship with a spouse, seeing the spouse in conjoint therapy or arranging separate therapy for the mate may be helpful. Spouses may not only limit the chances for optimal adjustment on the part of the patient by virtue of their own character structure, but they also may, at times, actively interfere with therapeutic progress. In the case of one man with agoraphobia, his wife became depressed every time his symptomatology disappeared. In another case of a depressed woman, the husband treated her with exquisite tenderness and solicitude as long as she remained depressed, and cruelly as soon as she was well. These are indeed "vicious" cycles with which individual therapy alone may not be able to deal. It is often the case that as people become older, they find themselves in increasingly fixed positions—life situations that may impose limitations on the degree to which analytic help can be utilized. Stone has discussed this problem very lucidly in his book, *The Psychoanalytic Situation* (1961).

However, many problems which arise within the psychotherapy situation, causing a block to progress, *can* be handled. The therapist may be able to introduce some other parameters. For instance, with a patient who is on the couch and may have reached a stalemate because anything that emerges is too anxiety-arousing, a tactical move, namely, having him sit up, is often sufficient to permit the therapy to move forward. On the other hand, a patient sitting up may be too conversational and too superficial. The analyst may have to ask him to lie down on the couch to permit less structured communication and to increase the level of anxiety so that more preconscious, and perhaps unconscious, material will emerge.

Under certain circumstances, such as discussed in relation to acting in the transference, an analyst might consider referring the patient to another analyst for a consultation. Seeing someone else in consultation may provide the primary therapist with added perspective vis-à-vis his working hypotheses and countertransference issues. It will, at the same time, provide the patient with another opinion and the opportunity to work through with the new therapist intractable transference problems with the primary therapist. In short, such a consultation may enable the patient and/or therapist to work through the stalemate.

If interventions such as those outlined do not break the stalemate, the analyst can suggest stopping the analysis for the time being. This will give the patient time to consolidate the gains that have been made, and give us the chance to see if the passage of time brings any clarification or shift in feelings. The analyst can set an arbitrary time for the patient to return, depending on the clinical situation, or the analyst can arrange to meet with the patient every two or three months as a type of monitoring, keeping open the possibility that the patient may resume treatment sometime in the future. There are two schools of thought concerning the termination date as a tactical response to a stalemate. The first demands that, once the analyst has set the date, he must abide by it. The second, more flexible position is that, when the termination date arrives, if the analytic process has begun to move well again, the analyst can tell the patient that, while discontinuing therapy had seemed appropriate at that earlier time, it might be better to continue now that the work has resumed. The analyst may even admit that this was a tactical move: "Setting a termination date seemed necessary to see if knowing there was a time limit would help you get the analysis out a rut and, indeed, you have worked through the problem. Now we can continue towards a much more satisfactory resolution. This was not a deception. If this tactic had not helped, analysis would have been terminated with the option to return if and when it might be more productive."

If stalemate persists despite all efforts, a termination date should indeed be honored. It is better to terminate by plan and as part of a therapeutic contract than to have therapy stop or fizzle out without proper working-through.

REFERENCES

GLOVER, E. *The Technique of Psychoanalysis*. New York: International Universities Press, 1955.

STONE, L. *The Psychoanalytic Situation*. New York: International Universities Press, 1961.

15. Dissociative Phenomena: Depersonalization, Derealization, Multiple Personality

Dissociative experiences can be very disruptive phenomena in the process of analysis or psychotherapy. In an attempt to cope with such disturbing experiences, the patient may act out impulsively, bizarrely, and even dangerously. Ultimately, he may want to break off treatment precipitously. Because depersonalization, derealization and the very rare syndrome of multiple personality have so often been identified with psychotic phenomena, the therapist also may become alarmed if these symptoms appear, diminishing his effectiveness and further negatively affecting the patient's behavior.

Dissociative phenomena may appear in a variety of forms, covering a wide spectrum of experience and behavior. The milder, more common forms often involve a combination of depersonalization and derealization—for example, the feeling of "freaking out," not being "with it," "being on the outside looking in," feeling that "the head is filled with cotton," or "enclosed by a glass wall." Some people (usually hysterics) with relatively mild feelings of derealization actually induce the experience, without knowing they are doing so; for example, if a person looks at an object close up while focusing on the horizon, the pupils become dilated and the close image appears fuzzy, unclear, out of focus. In turn, the fuzziness of the image on the retina induces some feelings of unreality, of being not related to or removed from the environment.

Other patients describe more disturbing phenomena, such as a

151

perception that everything is moving very far away. Objects appear as though they are being viewed through the wrong end of a telescope. The patient feels very strange and/or that the world around him is unreal. He or she may have very disturbing dreams in which figures and objects appear very small. Feelings of derealization often occur when people are in a large or strange city. Many people are afraid of New York for this reason. Walking on Wall Street, for example, with its very tall buildings and narrow streets, makes one feel like a figure in a Steig painting. College students often experience these feelings when away from home for the first time, suddenly separated from a familiar small town or country setting and a more structured life. Though they may report anxiety, on closer observation they are actually experiencing feelings of derealization and/or depersonalization. Certainly, anxiety itself can set off physiological phenomena, which in turn produce a dissociative experience. Hyperventilation, shallow fast breathing, causes the individual to exhale excessive carbon dioxide, thus reducing carbonic acid in the blood, and resulting in metabolic alkalosis. Hyperalkalinity, in turn, causes, among other things, spasms of the nuchal muscles which, along with the vestibular apparatus in the inner ear, are closely related to the sense of balance and orientation.

Currently, many people have dissociative experiences associated with taking a variety of drugs. These induce distortions of the environment, leading to feelings of derealization, and disturbances in body boundaries, leading to experiences of depersonalization. These side-effects of drugs like marijuana and hallucinogens (LSD, or mescaline, for example) are not necessarily limited to the time when the drug is pharmacologically active. "Flashbacks" may occur which cause a return to these disturbing experiences when the patient is otherwise stressed by certain circumstances, including, at times, anxiety-producing periods in analysis itself.

A more classical depersonalization phenomenon is having no sense of one's body or body parts. The mouth is most often involved and the hand next. The mouth is the organ obviously most closely associated with passive oral needs, as well as oral aggression, the wish to devour or be devoured. Thus, a numbness of the lips and mouth is a defense or splitting off of dependent passive wishes and/or oral aggression. As the hand is the executive organ for aggression, depersonalizing it or not feeling it is also a way of defending oneself against feelings of aggression by virtually splitting off one part of the body.

Depersonalization phenomena most often appear with the emergence of aggressive impulses, separation problems, and, less specifically, situations of stimulus hunger or deprivation.

At times of the emergence of powerful aggressive impulses which are disapproved of and which are then directed against the self, these impulses will set up a situation in which one part of the self looks at another part of the self with disapproving, aggressive connotations. The observing part of the self becomes quite critical of the estranged part. To a certain extent, this is a signal of some alarming condition, very similar to Freud's signal theory of anxiety. Here, the feeling of depersonalization serves as a signal that something is amiss, that there is a strong conflict between some impulse and the superego. This observation of part of the self that is unacceptable can be viewed in terms of Glover's (1930) concept of ego nuclei—the different parts of the ego which fuse when all goes well. When all does not go well, they do not fuse or do not fuse sufficiently, such that under stress the ego nuclei diffuse or dissociate. *Sybil,* a case of multiple personality, is an extreme case in point.

In multiple personality, separate ego states are expressed as though they are complete and different personalities. Under certain circumstances, if these separate ego states (other than the one currently being manifested) are remembered rather than repressed, one ego state may be critical of the other parts, and consequently, the individual will have feelings of estrangement from himself. The splitting of one part of the self from another part of the self and the subsequent disapproval of the one for the other can lead to acting-out. Although such extreme splitting is rarely seen, it does indeed exist and in some individuals can lead to major amnesias and/or something akin to multiple personality. It can also be a bridge to acting-out, where some unconscious ego state emerges and takes over in a programmed way. These phenomena are usually due to feelings of aggression. If the person is angry with those around him, these feelings of depersonalization are a way of removing oneself from the anger-inducing situation.

Similar disturbances occur when problems of separation appear, because in reality the analyst is unavailable due to illness or vacation, because the patient is going away, or because he has had a significant separation experience from an important someone in his own world, or is working through in analysis early problems of separation. In a dramatic instance of this nature, a patient suddenly developed peri-oral feelings of depersonalization. He had a very alarming sensation of deadness of the lips and mouth associated with the therapist's leaving for vacation and the threatened separation. He had experienced similar feelings when he went away to college, as well as when he left for school each day as a child. These feelings related to separation from his mother. His mother had suckled him until he was five. He had become an intelligent, nonpsychotic, professional man, but obviously and dramatically his history had left him with an oral problem. As a defensive maneuver, he physically experienced the separation via the mouth, and then experienced death under the impact of this separation, i.e., the feeling of deadness around the mouth, in effect making the statement: "Part of me is missing."

When suffering from feelings of depersonalization, patients often make urgent attempts to regain some sense of identity and to deal with this disturbing experience. Although psychotics suffer from depersonalization to a greater degree than less severely disturbed patients, nonpsychotics also may exhibit these symptoms and strive to deal with them in various ways. For example, a person may look obsessively into a mirror. When quite disturbed he will wonder if he is seeing his own face; he will grimace and touch the face. A patient with explosive anger reported that his face was numb. He felt that if he said anything his face would crack into bits. As the therapist and patient began to explore this problem, he developed symptoms which superseded the analytic treatment for about three weeks. He could not sleep because he began to scratch himself as soon as he got into bed. Analysts have often said to dermatologists that itching is a symptom of wanting to be loved. One "itches" to be touched. Thus, the scratching is an attempt to relieve the need. According to Lewin's (1946, 1948) theory about the breast as a dream screen, and Spitz's (1955) theory about the primal cave for cognitive perceptual purposes, falling asleep involves a feeling of separating oneself from the world, which could induce anxiety under certain circumstances, and lead to symptoms like the ones just described.

Another patient, nowhere near psychotic, dealt with his feeling of depersonalization, with "not being real," by smashing a windowpane with his bare hand. The feeling of being unreal was dispelled by the pain he experienced in smashing the window. Clarence Schulz (1975) of Sheppard Pratt Hospital noted that people who have difficulties with depersonalization often touch and slap themselves to increase proprioception. Standing in the shower is another way to deal with feelings of unreality and poor body boundaries. Some very disturbed people will spend three or four hours under the shower comforting themselves with body contact from the water and its feeling of enveloping warmth. These and similar manifestations may, of course, occur in psychotic regressions, which sometimes develop in the course of analysis or psychotherapy.

A related but broader phenomenon than depersonalization is "stimulus hunger." Many people require a great deal of stimulation. The nature and amount of activity a particular individual will choose to fulfill his stimulus hunger obviously reflect the degree or intensity of his hunger. Where a great deal of stimulus hunger is apparent, perhaps related to an underlying neurological problem, and a constant need for activity exists, some people use loud music, gum chewing, and general busy-ness as a defense, not in a dynamic sense, but rather a defense against depersonalization. Infants with a neurological problem such as MBD usually engage in knee/elbow rocking, head banging, etc., which later appear as ticks and/or hyperactivity. However, not all hyperactivity need be on a neurological basis. Overstimulation in infancy by either aggressive handling or excessive sexual handling can cause stimulus hunger.

In striking contrast, the experience of depersonalization, induced by many different means, is often found to be *pleasurable* by many people. Drug states are obvious examples, but depersonalization is also seen in children enjoying the feeling of being dizzy when whirled in the air or riding roller coasters, for example. Intense religious and esthetic experiences may also induce these feelings. Libidinization of anxiety occurs when endangering oneself, like hanging from a moving truck or climbing a mountain, becomes a pleasurable form of playing with anxiety. As long as the individual feels he can manage the anxiety through mastery, the ability to tolerate the anxiety is a pleasurable experience. A similar process takes place when seeing a drama or reading a piece of fiction. The willing suspension of disbelief enters in, but at the same time, the individual knows that it is simply the enactment or the telling of a drama. The feelings of unreality remain pleasant provided mastery over them is retained. Many people who purposefully induce feelings of unreality by taking certain drugs, watching a scary movie, etc., can do so in company with pleasurable results. But doing it alone is likely to produce dysphoria and perhaps panic.

MANAGEMENT

What can the analyst do when his patient experiences feelings of depersonalization? The major consideration for the therapist is to try to avoid *generating* these feelings in the patient. The analyst should be aware of the possibility of developing depersonalization experiences in the course of therapy if in the history-taking he finds that the patient has poor self-boundaries and experiences frequent déjà vu phenomena (the feeling of having seen something previously) and frequent déjà reconnu phenomena (the feeling of having experienced something previously). Such experiences may be due to mere physiologic changes resulting in a lag between actual perception and conscious registering of the data. They may also be induced by a variety of conditions such as anxiety and fatigue. It is possible that they also occur when some fantasized material matches a current perception or experience, and under the impact of anxiety, a certain disorientation and loss of boundaries take place. If the patient's history includes a symbiotic relationship with poor differentiation, the analyst should anticipate that in the course of the transference relationship, especially under the threat of separation, the patient is likely to relive this problem of insufficient self-boundaries and have feelings of unreality and depersonalization.

One patient who experienced such dissociative phenomena whenever feelings of separation came up had a husband who was very ill and who she feared might die. Angry and aggressive feelings would appear preconsciously as a result of her fear that he might "leave" her and she would then feel as if figures and objects were receding. This was her way of splitting off or removing herself from her own aggression. As a child she had once had the hypnogogic experience of seeing her parents disappearing into the wall. When she was 19, her boyfriend left her and she again had the experience of people fading away. If the analyst knows that the patient has poor self-boundaries, or if they are about to work something through that is likely to loosen self-boundaries and make the patient susceptible to this sort of disruptive experience, it is crucial that the analyst approach the conflict-laden material slowly, and perhaps predict (assisting mastery over the dissociative experience) that this sort of thing *might* occur.

In anticipation of such problems, the analyst may prefer to have the patient sit up. If the analyst has *not* anticipated these kinds of feelings and they in fact occur, then having the patient sit up would certainly be an appropriate maneuver in an attempt to dispel feelings of depersonalization. Patients being analyzed in the ordinary situation lying on a couch and facing an unstructured wall or ceiling have no field to depend on and preconscious (sometimes unconscious) processes emerge. This is Witkin's (1965) theory of field dependence and field independence. Lilly (1956) experienced feelings of depersonalization when he suspended himself in a tank under water without sight, smell, hearing, or the feeling of weight. Under analytic circumstances the analyst creates a degree of sensory deprivation which is likely to facilitate feelings of depersonalization in the patient. If this happens and it is too uncomfortable for the patient, the simple measure is to provide him with feedback, presenting the analyst's face and reactions and a clearly structured field.

If depersonalization occurs due to hyperventilation as a symptom of anxiety, the prescription of an anxiety-reducing drug will often alleviate the feelings. The small muscles between the ribs, the inter-costals, are most sensitive to excessive alkalinity in the blood due to overbreathing. Therefore, people will often get intercostal spasms which will cause them much concern about cardiac attacks and similar somatic problems. They will often complain that they do not know if they have pain or not. An anxiety-reducing drug should stop this problem.

REFERENCES

GLOVER, E. Grades of ego differentiation (1930). In *On the Early Development of the Mind.* New York: International Universities Press, 1956.

LEWIN, B. D. Sleep, the mouth, and the dream screen. *Psychoanal. Quart.,* 15:419-434, 1946.

LEWIN, B. D. Inferences from the dream screen. *Int. J. Psychoanal.,* 29:224-231, 1948.

LILLY, J. Mental effects of reduction of ordinary levels of physical stimuli on intact healthy persons. *Psychiatric Research Report,* 5:1-9, 1956.

MAY, P., WEXLER, M., SALKAN, J., & SCHOOP, T. Nonverbal techniques in the reestablishment of body image and self identity—a preliminary report. *Psychiat. Res. Rep.,* 16:68-82, 1963.

SCHULZ, C. G. Self and object differentiation as a measure of change in psychotherapy. In J. G. Gunderson and L. R. Mosher (Eds.), *Psychotherapy of Schizophrenia.* New York: Jason Aronson, 1975.

SPITZ, R. The primal cavity. In *The Psychoanalytic Study of the Child,* Vol. X. New York: International Universities Press, 1955.

WITKIN, H. Psychological differentiation and forms of pathology. *J. Abnormal Psychology,* 70, 1965.

16. Depression

A depression may appear as an intercurrent emergency in the analytic situation. This chapter, therefore, does not address the treatment of depression per se, or the emergency treatment of depression per se, but rather the treatment of depression as it arises within a specific frame of reference—as an emergency situation in an ongoing analysis or psychotherapy. This situation differs somewhat from the other two, though the dynamics are largely the same. Depression in the course of analysis occurs primarily for three reasons:

1) *The process of analysis itself has shaken the defenses* and led to the recovery of repressed material that, by itself, leads to a depression. However, the depression is greater than the analyst expected and more severe than the patient can tolerate.
2) *Reality factors* in the patient's life precipitate a depression of serious nature.
3) *The transference relationship* or the transference neurosis has induced a depressive reaction.

All depressions have certain dynamic factors in common, any one of which may play the major role in precipitating the depression. The main analytic theory involves the following propositions as basic to depression and its treatment:

159

1) *Problems of self-esteem.*
2) A *severe superego* in the presence of which
3) *Aggression* manifests itself mostly as *intra-aggression.*
4) A feeling of *loss*—of love, of a love object, of part of oneself, of possessions, of self-esteem.
5) A feeling of *disappointment,* which
6) Edith Jacobson (1971) has also related to a feeling of having been the victim of *deception.*
7) Instead of the narrower concept of *orality,* I like to speak of *stimulus hunger* (Bellak & Berneman, 1971) and the fact that the depressed personality tends to be more dependent on all kinds of positive input than other people, possibly for some physiological reasons.
8) The depressed personality, in a broader sense, is more dependent on external *narcissistic nutrients,* which in turn are obviously linked with problems of self-esteem orality and object relations.
9) The outstanding defense mechanism in depression (as well as in elation) is usually *denial* (Lewin, 1950).
10) All of the above nine factors relate in a general sense to *object relations* and their disturbances, the specific vicissitudes of which must be understood in terms of internalization, object representation, and self-representation. This is most succinctly discussed by Edith Jacobson (1971). Dynamically, the object relations of the depressed are *usually anaclitic,* passive-dependent, receptive and *ambivalent,* consistent with the above.

The systematic treatment of depression is predicated on the proposition that the rank order of importance of these ten variables must first be determined. The necessary therapeutic interventions may then be designed to deal with each of the rank-ordered factors in a given sequence, with the appropriate methods of intervention and areas of intervention. With regard to areas of intervention, the therapist may, in one patient, address himself initially to the loss of self-esteem, and only after that turn to his aggresion, intra-aggression and severe superego. With another patient, it will be more appropriate to primarily address his severe superego and the intra-aggression, and turn only later to orality and the feelings of deception and other factors. The method(s) of intervention may be interpretation, catharsis, mediate catharsis, drive repression, intellectualization or others (Bellak & Small, 1978).

The analyst has done an important piece of work if he can relate the intercurrent depression in the analysis to the patient's prior history, keeping in mind the ten variables mentioned above.

The following treatment parameters form a very useful guide to the treatment of depression occurring as an intercurrent emergency in the analytic situation.

1) *Problems of Self-Esteem*

Problems of self-esteem should be treated by exploring the life history of the patient with regard to self-esteem or the lack of it (introjects, traumas, defects, level of aspiration).

Recent insults to self-esteem must also be carefully investigated. The therapist should relate common denominators in past history and recent participating events inside and outside the analytic process for the purposes of interpretation, insight, and working-through. The interventions should focus on structural problems of self-esteem. It goes without saying that, in all these interventions and those to follow, the analyst must take pains to *treat the patient with dignity*. He should offer support and point out areas in a patient's life consonant with high self-esteem.

In addition, in an attempt to reduce the differential between unrealistic expectations (expectations which are too low or too high) and reality, one must examine in detail the nature of ego ideals, the level of aspiration and the soundness of defenses. Here the subdivisions of self-esteem promulgated by Bibring (1953) are useful to keep in mind as a guide for specific therapeutic intervention. Bibring advanced the theoretical understanding of self-esteem and its impairment from the narrow concept that problems in self-esteem relate only to oral problems to encompass the frustration of other aspirations, e.g., at the anal or the phallic level of development. He characterized depressions related to frustrations at the anal level of development with the failure of aspirations to be good and loving, not to be dirty, hostile or defiant. In the case of depressions where phallic frustrations play a role, the wish to be superior, great, strong and secure would appear in depressions as a feeling of inadequacy, inferiority, and ineffectiveness. He stressed that the general common denominator in all depressions, regardless of their relationship to a particular level of libidinal fixation, was the pervasive feeling of helplessness. Transference interpretations which seem especially relevant to this problem should obviously be a part of the treatment of low self-esteem.

2) A Severe Superego

A severe superego should be treated by understanding what components make it necessary to deflect aggression against the self. Treatment should include exploring the superego formation, its constituents, its manifestations, and the contemporary situation, and finding common denominators between the past and the present, by interpretation, insight, and working-through.

To treat a severe superego, I recommend the use of *mediate catharsis,* as described previously (Bellak & Small, 1978; this volume, Chapter 4). Mediate catharsis is a term which I like to use when I express emotionally charged propositions for the patient. For instance, with a depressed patient with a severe superego and a good deal of aggression, I may say, "Certainly if the foreman had done that to me, I would have kicked him." In this instance, I am expressing sentiments for the patient which might be too strong for his sensitive superego; by virtue of my saying them, I take the superego responsibility for them. I hope that I also convey to the patient that if an authority such as the therapist can permit himself such an aggressive thought, that it may not be so unacceptable. Identification and introjection of the therapist as a more benign part of the superego then play an important role in this part of the therapeutic process.

Using *catharsis,* the therapist encourages the patient to express his feelings, while pointing out their denial.

When a severe superego is contributing to a depression, it is important to examine any projections within the transference situation, contrasting them to the therapist's neutrality.

3) *Aggression and Intra-Aggression*

The treatment of intra-aggression as a main variable should be pursued by studying the life history and contemporary precipitating events inside or outside the analysis to determine the primary object of the aggression historically, as well as the current object of aggression. One has to relate the internalized objects against whom aggression was and is directed because of previous disappointment, deception, etc., to contemporary objects. In doing this, the therapist should make the patient aware of the fact that the contemporary object causing his current trauma, such as the love object, has been apperceptively distorted by his past experiences, such as with parental figures.

Aggression may also be directed against self-representations; that is, one part of the self directs criticism against another part of the self. One must deal with the fact that self-esteem regulation plays a major role in depressions. Differences between the ego ideal—to be great, to be strong, to be clean—and the sense of self with regard to these goals also play an important role in intra-aggression.

4) *A Feeling of Loss (of Love, of a Love Object, of Part of Oneself, of Possessions, of Self-Esteem)*

Intercurrent life experiences, transference phenomena or the reliving of past traumata may precipitate feelings of loss of love. Such a feeling of loss should be treated by examining the life history, particularly with regard to early losses, eliciting current precipitating events relating to a loss, and helping the patient obtain insight by working through the current loss in relation to past traumas. It is necessary to examine the general nature of object relationships, especially excessive dependent-passive demands which facilitate a feeling of disappointment. Careful attention must also be paid to the need for love, specifically in the transference situation.

5, 6) *Feelings of Disappointment and Deception*

Depression primarily related to disappointment and deception should be treated by following Jacobson's (1971) concept of disappointment being related to the feeling of having been deceived. The life history should be studied especially for previous events relating to the feeling of disappointment and deception.

The precipitating event which triggered the depression should be examined for evidences of disappointment and deception, and common denominators established between the earlier experiences of disappointment and feelings of having been deceived and contemporary feelings of this same nature, for the purposes of interpretation, insight, and working-through. The transference relationship should be vigilantly observed from this standpoint.

It will be necessary to deal with the anger against the disappointing love object. Very often, unconscious anger against the therapist will play the major role in a transitory depression.*

7) *Orality and Stimulus Hunger*

The treatment of orality and stimulus hunger as a main variable in depression should be pursued by examining the patient's life history for evidences of the need for oral supply and other stimuli, and the depressive reaction when they are not made available. This can be pointed out to the patient. In addition, common denominators will be readily found in the transference relationship.

In the treatment of this variable of depression, a broad concept of oral needs is preferred. For this reason, I prefer to use the term "stimulus hunger." This permits one to include the treatment of not only the classical oral needs, but also the need for love generally, and the need for input, sound, light and human contact which is manifested in hypomanic situations and latent in depressions. See,

---

* Jacobson (1971) suggested that it is part of the superego, formed to a large extent by internalization of parental figures, etc., which brings about guilt and depression. In distinction, she felt that one part of the self being critical of another part is the basic mechanism in depersonalization.

for this purpose, my paper with Berneman (1971) and the theory of depression outlined therein.

In this context, Bertram Lewin's (1950) oral triad—the need to devour, the wish to be devoured, and the wish to sleep—has to be looked for and dealt with therapeutically.

8) *Narcissism*

Depressed patients usually have more secondary narcissism than (other) neurotic patients. Their object relations are usually primarily of an anaclitic nature. Their narcissistic needs are closely related to the orality and stimulus hunger discussed above. One can, in fact, speak of their need for *narcissistic nutrients*. Their narcissism, however, is also specifically related to their pathological forms of self-esteem regulation.

As a main variable in depression, narcissism should be treated by examining the patient's attempts to regulate intake of stimuli of all kinds. In this instance, a depressed person may be compared to the poikilotherm animal (popularly misnamed cold-blooded because, if exposed to low external temperature, its body temperature goes down). Similarly, if the depressive individuals have chilling emotional experiences, their self-esteem decreases catastrophically, and their need for external narcissistic supplies increases sharply. The nondepressive personality, on the other hand, is more like the homoiothermic animal, whose cerebral "homeostat" maintains a constant narrow range of temperature despite wide external fluctuations.

In his attempt to regulate this stimulus hunger, the depressed patient often has to walk a difficult line between overstimulation and understimulation, between being overreactive and tense or being hypoactive and depressed. Analysis of defenses frequently exacerbates these problems during treatment.

Education and planning of the patient's life are part of the therapeutic task. The treatment of excessive narcissism involves analyzing the excessive need to be loved due to a lack of good introjects. It is the resulting feeling of emptiness which is often perceived as coming from the outside and is related to the previously discussed need for input, feelings of low self-esteem, poor object relationships, and taking the self as one's own love object. This is discussed in detail by Jacobson (1971).

The stimulus hunger, as well as the lability, may in some cases be related to a biochemical disturbance.

9) Denial

The treatment of denial as the major defense mechanism in depression should be addressed by examining the life history for previous occurrences of denial and whether they were followed by subsequent depressions or elations. Denial as the outstanding mechanism in affective disorders (especially the hypomanic state) was most extensively discussed by Bertram Lewin (1950). He described the thought processes involved as *centrifugal*. This process can indeed be most interestingly observed in truly manic patients, especially if one tries to have them face their denied affect. In depressed patients, the traumatic event—the disappointment, deception, or enraging event —is often denied. This is so in the case of many depressions which are considered endogenous by nondynamic psychiatrists, simply because the precipitating event was denied by the patient and not clearly evident in the life history as obtained by the dynamically uninformed. This is, of course, different in clearly reactive depressions, where only the relationship to the internalized object is denied. In either case, the therapeutic task, as usual in psychoanalytic psychotherapy, is to establish continuity where there is discontinuity and to point out the denied affect. This alone will frequently rapidly reverse a depression.

One should use both mediate catharsis, as previously described, and direct catharsis, which is very useful in this instance. Limited as it is, the use of ventilation can be very helpful in the lifting of depression after the cathartic interpretation of the denied affect and the denied events. It is important that one help the patient to express his rage at the person precipitating the current depression, as well as at the related introjects. Of course, the rage will often be expressed in the transference situation.

10) *Object Relations*

Disturbances in object relations, as a main variable in depression, should be treated by examining the life history for the nature of object relations. In the depressed, object relations are often of an anaclitic nature, with oral clinging playing a predominant role. The narcissism and the need for narcissistic supplies have already been pointed out, as well as orality in a broad sense. In the history of the depressed, oral deprivation, or especially a mixture of overindulgence and deprivation, plays an important role.

Critical parents are often the cause of an excessive level of aspiration, and the correspondingly low self-estimate. The need to please others, with the nearly built-in conditions for failing, plays a major role. In the seriously depressed, symbiotic relationships, with concomitant difficulties in self-boundaries, are prevalant.

The analyst must clearly understand which factor plays the primary role in the patient's depression. A little depression is part of the human condition, but in a significant depression the analyst will want to review for himself how and when the depression began in relation to processes in the analysis and in the patient's life. Then the analyst should engage primarily in interpretation, i.e., pointing out the common denominators he sees between the precipitating loss of self-esteem, or the feeling of deception or disappointment, or whatever factor is salient in the current analytic or life situation, and earlier feelings of this nature.

Aside from analyzing and interpreting, the analyst can introduce other parameters, such as being more supportive, having the patient sit up, being willing to discuss neutral subjects for a few minutes as a form of relating and giving. Various drugs may be a useful adjunct for a period of time. They constitute an enabling condition for carrying on successful psychotherapy.

REFERENCES

BELLAK, L. & BERNEMAN, N. A Systematic view of depression. *Am. J. Psychotherapy*, 25 (3):385-393, 1971.

BELLAK, L. & SMALL, L. *Emergency Psychotherapy and Brief Psychotherapy.* Second Edition. New York: Grune & Stratton, 1978.

BIBRING, E. The mechanism of depression. In P. Greenacre (Ed.), *Affective Disorders.* New York: International Universities Press, 1953.

JACOBSON, E. *Depression: Comparative Studies of Normal, Neurotic and Psychotic Conditions.* New York: International Universities Press, 1971.

LEWIN, B. *The Psychoanalysis of Elation.* New York: W. W. Norton, 1950.

17. Suicidal Danger

DEFINITIONS

Few people, if any, become acutely suicidal in psychoanalysis or psychotherapy due to the process itself. Usually such patients have been seriously suicidal earlier in their lives. In such a case, almost anything may serve as a trigger. For instance, one patient, identifying with the libretto, attempted suicide after seeing the opera Carmen, having felt jilted by his wife. This was the immediate precipitating factor, but a careful anamnesis revealed that he had made attempts previously. The therapist must know whether his patient has ever been suicidal in the past and, if so, he must keep the potential danger of its reoccurence in mind. He must be prepared to modify his treatment technique and to deal with suicidal tendencies if they should become acute during the course of analysis.

ANAMNESIS AND ASSESSMENT

The most important criterion for the possibility of suicide is a previous serious attempt. Serious attempts are those in which the patient had a high probability of dying and was discovered by an unpredictable coincidence, or where he managed to survive a truly life-threatening situation. These cases stand out in distinction to someone who took a few pills or slashed his or her wrists superficially. Such attempts are usually more in the nature of a gesture, but also should not be disregarded. In general, the more concretely someone plans suicide, e.g., leaving detailed instructions about a will, having a specific scenario in terms of method, time, place, etc., the greater the risk. Shneidman (1980), who has made a study of suicide notes, underscores the portentousness of concreteness. The more concrete the plans that someone has made for committing suicide, the more cause for concern. However, absence of plans is no reason for ignoring suicidal tendencies; some patients who attempt suicide only as a gesture may "accidentally" overdo it and succeed only too well.

A family history of suicide and/or a history of violent acting-out in other forms, especially in childhood, is ominous. People who killed pets or injured playmates as children are prime risks. This stands to reason dynamically, since intra-aggression and aggression against others often seem to be correlated, the common denominator being a high level of aggression and poor impulse control. An example which illustrates this is that of Goebbels, the Nazi criminal, who was personally responsible for the torture and death of thousands. In defeat, he killed his wife and children, and then committed suicide.

To understand and treat suicide, one should keep in mind the points discussed in the treatment of depression and the therapy of acting-out. After all, most, although by no means all, suicidal people are depressed, and suicide frequently shares many of the characteristics of acting-out. Very acutely suicidal people, those whom Shneidman (1980) considers to have high lethality and high perturbation, require special treatment measures, as discussed later. In Shneidman's scheme, what he calls lethality, the acute suicidalness, is of limited duration. Unless one can "do it" then and there, it's no "fun." Along with acting-out, the impulse or urge to commit suicide is often associated with a need for immediacy.

Depressed people are not necessarily the only ones or even the most likely ones to be serious suicidal dangers. Panic often plays the primary role. For instance, former U.S. Defense Secretary Forrestal, in a panic, thought that the Russians were after him and jumped out of a window to escape them. One patient had the delusional and hallucinatory fear of being caught in a net and stabbed while helplessly entangled. Suicide seemed a reasonable way out of such torture. One young man had tortuously nagging, obsessive and delusional symptoms, and finally, in a desperate attempt to end them, threw himself down a stairwell. Another patient had "command" hallucinations urging him to jump out of a window. Such voices are almost invariably the voices of the superego, and people suffering from such hallucinations are first-rank suicide risks.

Schizophrenic patients can be in a variety of panics, such as those of a paranoid or homosexual nature. Or they may suffer from the terror of the awareness of disintegration. The cognitive changes that accompany their illness may so frighten them that they will attempt suicide. These kinds of panics are often more lethal than depression. In some severely dissociated patients, one might see what looks like "depression," but might be more properly called desperation. One man who was diagnosed as schizophrenic suffered mainly from minimal brain dysfunction, and was desperate about his inability to control his impulses. It took all his energy to maintain control, such that he could scarcely perform any work. He was a bright young man whose struggles were heartbreaking to see. This individual was a serious suicide risk.

An additional and often curious factor which should be kept in mind when assessing suicidal risk is the individual's *concept of death*. Surprisingly, these concepts vary greatly. Many people, primarily those with a great deal of orality, seem to have the idea that death is a form of sleep, some sort of refreshing repose from which they will awaken with all their problems having been resolved. When attempting suicide, such people will most often ingest toxins, in keeping with their oral organization. In our culture, these agents will most often be sleeping pills. This suicidal risk group would include a large number of depressed people, quite in accordance with Lewin's concept of the oral triad, namely the wish to sleep, to devour, and to be devoured.

The availability of instruments for suicide, as well as cultural factors, plays a role in the particular method chosen. For instance, the oral route is most likely to be the one chosen by women, while more men than women use guns and knives. Gas used in cooking or fumes from an automobile are methods frequently chosen in this culture, since seemingly painless means are preferred. Most people don't relish the thought of hurting themselves badly, in the sense of inflicting physical pain, even though they may not mind killing themselves. An odd extension of this wish to avoid self-harm while annihilating oneself is the old coroner's rule that if the bullet passed through the jacket, it was probably murder, not suicide. Ironically, not wishing to damage valuable clothing is in this sense actually denying the life-destroying nature of the act. Most suicides would first take off the jacket and carefully fold it, or at least push it aside.

Some people actually fantasize themselves surviving the suicide and standing at their graveside laughing happily at all those people who are sorry that weren't nicer to the deceased.

MANAGEMENT

As in all instances, a careful anamnesis is important: If there are any suggestions of suicidal tendencies, the analysis of any factors which might relate to them has to be carefully handled. These factors would include aggression, problems of self-esteem, and the specific recovery of traumatic events in the course of the analysis.

If there is any reason to suspect suicidal notions or fantasies, it is essential that the analyst insist that the patient spell them out, in as much concrete detail as possible. The explicit statement of all suicidal notions may have a cathartic effect and facilitate reality testing by both patient and therapist.

If the patient is extremely suicidal, and has what Shneidman would call "high lethality," *one has to abandon therapeutic neutrality*. It is necessary to be supportive, reassure the patient, make him realize that there are other choices available besides the one of self-destruction, and assure him that one will be available around the clock. With the patient's permission, if possible, family members should be informed of the situation. The therapist should acquaint the patient with the availability of crisis lines and services in the community, just in case the analyst himself is not accessible.

When extreme lethality is over, one has to reanalyze the loss of therapeutic neutrality and anything else that may be relevant. Then, one can again proceed with more ordinary measures, which are in essence a combination of what has been discussed for the management of depression and of acting-out.

Among other things, the patient's specific fantasies concerning suicide need to be examined in detail. Any unrealistic notions about death should be clarified, for example, the fantasy that one will really survive suicide and wake up as if from a sleep. Suicidal patients suffer from "tunnel vision" and only see one particular solution. It is therefore important to show them that there are other options.

Analytically speaking, it is essential to understand which introject the aggression is meant for; that is, one must understand to which *earlier introject* the *contemporary figure* who provides the disappointment, deception, or other insult, is related. In this context, *transference sentiments,* i.e., hostility towards the therapist, are frequently responsible for suicidal ideas, and should be identified and interpreted.

If anamnesis has established some suicidal tendencies, it is very useful for the therapist to know who the patient's internist or general practitioner is and establish some liaison, just in case an acute suicidal attempt is made. In this event, the medical person will be much better equipped than the therapist to deal with the life-threatening emergency. Generally, it is very useful for anybody engaged in the treatment of relatively severely disturbed people to have a close working relationship with a hospital so that the patient can be briefly hospitalized if necessary to tide him over a particular danger. Active working-through can be done in that protective setting. Of course, pharmacotherapy and, in very rare instances, ECT, may be indicated.

If there is a serious concern about the possibility of suicide, one should not hesitate to take appropriate measures. Attempting to carry all the responsibility oneself is likely to produce considerable anxiety and the communication of that anxiety may only alarm the patient and make him more suicidal. Therefore, if one has an acute enough concern, it may be useful, with the patient's agreement or, if necessary, without it, to call a relative to the office and arrange for him to accompany the patient home. It may even be necessary to temporarily abandon therapeutic neutrality and take the patient home or to a hospital oneself.

Insurance problems in suicide can be especially troublesome. In some cases, the company may not be liable in the case of suicide, but may be liable in the instance of accidental death. If apparent suicide indeed occurs, it will be important for the therapist to consult an attorney immediately, and have him present when there is any kind of legal conference with members of the family or with an insurance company. This is important not only in terms of the questions of his own responsibility, but also for the protection of the profession. A deceased person still has certain rights of privacy, and disclosure of clinical material should be made only after consultation with attorneys and one's professional society.

REFERENCES

LEWIN, B. D. Sleep, the mouth and the dream screen. *Psychoanal. Quart.*, 15:419-434, 1946.

SHNEIDMAN, E. Psychotherapy with suicidal patients. In T. B. Karasu and L. Bellak (Eds.), *Specialized Techniques in Individual Psychotherapy*. New York: Brunner/ Mazel, 1980.

18. Psychotic Manifestations

DEFINITIONS

Psychotic episodes can occur under the stress of psychoanalytic or psychotherapeutic work, especially if a patient has a tendency toward them. When the defenses weaken and repressed conflicts emerge, the reactivation of problems in the transference neurosis can contribute significantly to a psychotic episode, a transference psychosis perhaps. But it is doubtful that psychotic episodes occur solely as the result of psychotherapeutic maneuvers.

ANAMNESIS AND ASSESSMENT

Careful anamnesis will alert the therapist to the fact that psychotic episodes have occurred before and that there is a reasonable possibility that they might recur. Patients who develop psychotic episodes in the course of treatment may reconstitute on a much better level after the psychosis and may, in fact, be able to analyze areas which were not previously available, thus improving the general therapeutic result. Nevertheless, psychotic regressions should not be viewed as desirable. Some analysts believe that psychosis is the price of engaging in psychoanalytic maneuvers for the sake of reconstituting on a better adaptive level. It is, however, neither good technique nor justifiable treatment to take any more than the very least risk of a psychotic regression in the course of treatment.

One can never be sure that a psychosis will resolve satisfactorily. Also, chances of a severe dissociative experience are too great, leaving a tendency for repeated dissociation.

MANAGEMENT

There are a number of psychodynamic techniques the analyst can apply if the patient experiences a psychotic episode.

The analyst should be able to trace the precipitating event(s), both in the therapy and in the patient's personal life. He can then use a few well chosen cathartic interpretations that will decrease the drive pressure, or the superego pressure, and thus lessen the strength of the conflict. A patient had suffered a severe blow to his self-esteem. Instead of feeling angry about what had been done to him, he responded by developing a Christ-like attitude, with acute cosmic delusions. He could do good deeds for everyone, understand what people and animals were thinking, and commune with the entire universe. These reactions were largely the result of the denial of the loss of self-esteem and of the anger. Analyzing the initial upsetting event and its effects on him, especially in terms of his attempt at denial and reaction formation, promptly resolved the psychotic regression.

The manic reaction in a psychotic regression always involves denial. The patient's typical manner of talking has been described as centrifugal—all thoughts avoid the central area, which is too painful. For example, the individual will attempt to make himself feel and appear big because he feels very small. These are the psychodynamics of the manic reaction, regardless of the biochemical factors that might possibly be involved. If the analyst understands what the patient is denying, he can change the manic reaction into a depression and treat the problem on that basis. This is essentially the interpretation of psychotic phenomena as forms of defense.

Alternatively, the analyst can support defenses. For example, when intolerable aggression contributes to the psychotic regression, the analyst can decrease the conflict by affecting the force of either the superego or the drive, since in essence the conflict arises out of the opposing forces of the superego and the drive. The analyst can strengthen the superego and therefore decrease the drive, or weaken the drive and therefore strengthen the superego, depending on which is more appropriate.

For the duration of the psychotic episode, the analyst serves as the patient's auxiliary ego, especially with regard to reality testing. He also offers support and education. He gives a clear uncritical account of what processes are taking place, making them at least intellectually understandable to the patient. If the patient has been on the couch, the analyst should ask him to sit up, thus providing a feedback mechanism, rather than continue to place the patient in a situation of perceptual isolation. Having the patient lie on the couch makes reality testing more difficult and facilitates the emergency of more preconscious and unconscious material, which should be avoided if the danger of psychotic regression is present.

The analyst should consider subsidiary measures in dealing with psychotic episodes. He should actively intervene if the patient is disturbed by a specific reality situation which constitutes a form of overload. He should suggest that the patient remove himself from that particular situation, for instance, an especially pathogenic family setting.

The analyst should see that the patient gets enough sleep. Psychotic episodes are an indication for sleeping pills or tranquilizers, although the analyst must be careful the patient is not given enough medication to be able to kill himself. The analyst should see to it that the patient avoids overloads of any kind. This is analogous to putting the arm in a splint when fractured. The analyst splints the ego for the time being, until the psychotic episode passes.

Psychotropic drugs can also be used to deal with intercurrent psychotic episodes. As long as the analyst returns to the episode and reanalyzes it when the patient has reconstituted, drugs do not interfere with the analytic process. In fact, the analyst should not wait too long to use drugs if he is not successful with some simple psychotherapeutic maneuvers.

If one is dealing primarily with a transference psychosis, one may wish to utilize an auxiliary therapist, as discussed under transference problems. Such an auxiliary therapist has the main function of diluting and otherwise dealing with the overwhelming transference problems. Not infrequently, a therapist of the opposite sex to the primary therapist is especially useful.

III. Extrinsic Conditions

Analysis operates ordinarily under "average expectable conditions" and so do other forms of psychotherapy. Regrettably, reality is not always that obliging and at times introduces more or less disturbing intercurrent events.

Unlike some of the intrinsic conditions which can be anticipated by a careful anamnesis, extrinsic conditions have to be dealt with as they arise. The only preparation for them is to have some general ideas about the basic variables involved in some of the changes and complications in everyday life which occur with some frequency, and may thus occur in patients in the course of treatment.

To these belong hopefully joyous ones such as marriage and childbirth, and upsetting ones such as job loss, illness, loss of a loved one and others.

Emergency psychotherapy has been a special interest of mine for three decades. This part of the book draws on some of my past experiences with it.

19. Actual or Threatened Intercurrent Physical Illness in the Patient

Interventions other than those commensurate with strictly analytical processes are often indicated because the analyst or therapist must deal with the real person, not a concept. If a patient develops a major illness, for instance, the immediate therapeutic goal must be realigned. Psychoanalysis becomes psychotherapy, at least for the time being. The analyst becomes actively involved, focusing on helping the patient cope with the psychological aspects and problems of the threatening illness.

ANAMNESIS AND ASSESSMENT

It is essential to explore the meaning of the illness, whether the problem is major or minor. The same illness will have quite different meanings to different people, in realistic and/or symbolic ways. A coronary infarct may realistically mean a change of occupation and financial status to one person, and make little difference in those areas to another. Symbolically, it may mean punishment for unconscious death wishes toward someone else to the first person and a loss of masculinity to the second. For some people, the main threat of any illness lies in the general fear of passivity, which may in some situa-

181

tions be based mainly on their worst fantasies. In other cases this fear is more realistically based on actual enforced passivity. Narcissistic injury may also play a major role. In a woman, this could manifest itself in a concern with beauty, and in a man, a concern with "machismo." In each case, the illness needs to be analyzed with regard to both the realistic and the symbolic meaning.

Not infrequently, the meaning of an illness may be inappropriately derived from a historical source: If the patient's mother suffered from rheumatic heart disease, the patient who has had an infarct may confound one condition with the other intellectually, as well as inappropriately identify with the significant other unconsciously.

Often, the affected organ becomes overcathected in the course of an illness. When the liver becomes diseased, for example, it will tend to loom very large in the patient's body image, like the New Yorker's concept of the United States which envisions the city covering two-thirds of the map. This conceptual distortion can be easily demonstrated if the analyst has the patient draw the body, including the affected organ or part (Bellak, 1952).

During the course of an illness, a relationship is often established between the patient and his diseased organ, similar to that of a parent to a child. The diseased organ takes the role of the sick child who needs care. This is apparent in phrases like "My stomach can't tolerate. . . ." The diseased part is first anthropomorphized. Then it is spoken of as having an independent life, with independent preferences and sensitivities. If the situation is transitory, this will resolve itself when the emergency is over. But if it is a chronic illness, it is important to analyze the excessive anthropomorphization and narcissistic over-cathexis of the disease, the organ, or the body part. The more serious the affliction, however, the more complex the analyst's problems in dealing with it.

MANAGEMENT

Reality testing is the analyst's basic task in helping the patient deal with intercurrent physical illness. The analyst may have to acquaint himself with the particular aspects of the patient's disease so that he can help the patient understand the nature of his illness by educating and clarifying any misconceptions. Primary care physicians rarely take the time and trouble to have their patients fully understand the nature of the illness and/or treatments.

Most people have a very poor understanding of anatomy, physiology and pathology. With coronary patients, for example, it is often important to discuss how repair takes place by the formation of new blood vessels, collaterals which carry the blood that the damaged vessels can no longer carry, in order to nourish and renew the heart muscle. These collateral arteries are encouraged in their development by appropriate exercise. Thus the analyst can help the patient avoid becoming a chronic invalid because of excessive fear and passivity.

Asking the patient to draw pictures of his bodily affliction will help to clarify the patient's concept of it. He might draw a picture of a coronary with an embolus in the artery that looks like a phallus attacking it. He might draw a picture of a malignancy that looks like a gaping mouth with teeth, revealing cannibalistic fantasies about the malignancy.

One patient, who was terribly disgusted by the idea of having a gastric ulcer, reacted with nausea to the idea of having fluid oozing in his stomach. He found the gastric ulcer particularly unappetizing because he equated it with the leg ulcers he had seen on an aging relative.

The analyst should become acquainted with the patient's personal physician. Some physicians are very stiff and hesitate to talk about the illness because they feel somehow threatened by it, dismissing the task of educating and informing the patient about his condition as not part of their work. They feel that they are paid to perform the procedure, not to explain it. Assuming that the patient has a reasonable physician, the therapist should introduce himself and explain that he would like to know as much as possible about the patient's illness, in order to be able to help him with it emotionally. What is the patient's current physical state? What is the prognosis? What drugs is he taking, in what amount, and what are their side-effects? The analyst should inform himself about the patient's medical problem(s) generally and should maintain a close liaison with the physician in case special problems arise. If the patient develops dizziness, for example, it may be due to hyperventilation because he is unhappy with his wife, or it may be due to the high blood pressure from which he chronically suffers.

If, during the course of analysis, a patient develops a physical illness and does not have a physician, the analyst can suggest a few he knows and trusts, and with whom he has a comfortable relationship. This may violate therapeutic neutrality, but may well be worth it if it avoids incompetence and harmful interventions. As in all instances, any active role of the analyst has to be analyzed and reanalyzed when necessary.

REFERENCES

BELLAK, L. (Editor and Contributor). *The Psychology of Physical Illness: Psychiatry Applied to Medicine, Surgery and the Specialties.* New York: Grune & Stratton, 1952.

20. Facing Major Surgery

Surgery is often a psychological trauma as well as a physical one. If the operation is major and occurs in the course of therapy, the analyst often needs to serve as liaison between the patient, his family, the surgeon, and the participating hospital staff. He may serve as receptor for the anxieties of all involved parties and can help open paths of communication which otherwise might remain closed (Rosen, 1952).

Often a patient will be reluctant to discuss some aspects of surgery with his surgeon, including any possible misgivings about his surgery, because he feels dependent upon that physician for his very life.

The therapist can determine whether the patient anticipates unrealistic benefits or harm as consequences of his operation and can provide appropriate counsel to patient and surgeon. Surgeons sometimes appear overly casual about the proposed surgery and do not always divulge possible unpleasant results or side-effects of the operation for fear of discouraging or frightening the patient or his family. In such a case, one faces a potential crisis and the analyst must, with everybody's consent, discuss all possible facets of the operation with the patient.

SOME GENERAL PROPOSITIONS

The analyst or therapist should explore the patient's general and specific fears of surgery. The fears of dying by surgery may differ from the fears of dying in general. Notions of being cut open are taken from both childhood fantasies and unfortunate real life experiences, for example, a particularly traumatic tonsillectomy as a child.

Similarly, specific kinds of surgery stimulate rather standard reactions. A prostate operation will usually arouse fears of impotence and reawaken old castration anxieties. Breast operations, on the other hand, are often perceived as threats to a patient's femininity. Legitimate concerns about the cosmetic aspects, as well as possible complications of the operation, need to be discussed with the patient.

Statistically, abdominal operations were (until the advent of open heart surgery) seen as the major surgical threat and had the highest incidence of postoperative psychoses. The analyst must explore the patient's fantasies about what procedures will be performed in the abdomen. Amputations are the third in line of procedures which precipitate psychoses.

Specific operations may be particularly threatening to some people for idiosyncratic reasons. A female patient became psychotic after a hemorrhoidectomy. This patient had been able to have orgasms only by anal stimulation. Hemorrhoidectomy was seen as a sexual act as well as a terrible threat to her sexuality. Postoperative delusions and hallucinations in this and similar instances usually involve the surgeon and frequently have a paranoid flavor.

Not to be forgotten is the need for the analyst to explore the patient's specific fears concerning anesthesia. Many such fears arise and may be extremely troubling. Patients fear sensations of choking, burning in the throat and lungs struggling for air. Some people prefer spinal anesthesia because they would rather remain awake to keep an eye on things, including their surgeon. They may feel better staying conscious as a reflection of concerns about perhaps not waking up again, or especially strong fears of passivity. Other people don't want to know and prefer intravenous sedation followed by inhalation anesthesia.

As always, the analyst remains in the neutral role as much as possible. However, if he has reason to worry about some aspect of the medical proceedings—for example, if he suspects that the patient is in the hands of an incompetent or unscrupulous physician—the analyst may be required to step out of the strictly analytic role and suggest that the patient consult another surgeon for a second opinion. He should not let his patient come to unnecessary harm. This hierarchy of goals requires that the therapist not hesitate to temporarily give up his strictly neutral attitude and adopt one which respects the compelling reality at hand. The relatively healthier the patient, the less variation of the analytic technique necessary; the less serious the situation, the less change is necessary as well. The more severe these variables, the more the analyst must modify his function.

While the patient is hospitalized, the more intact the patient and the less serious the surgery, the less the analyst has to be involved, if at all. The more disturbed the patient and the more severe the medical-surgical condition, the more appropriate it is for the analyst to take an active role. Aside from phoning the patient, he may wish to visit the patient in the hospital. If the patient is in critical condition, it is reasonable for the analyst to make several visits as a bedside therapist, to help the patient with the current crisis. This may indeed introduce situations that cause trouble in the transference relationship later on, but they can be analyzed at that point. If the patient is in danger of dying, it is more important to help him with that acute reality than it is to worry about the effects on the transference relationship. Under certain circumstances, the analyst, after discussion with the patient, may prefer to delegate therapeutic responsibility to another analyst or therapist in the hospital if he, the primary analyst, cannot be available or foresees major transference problems with this patient which would outweigh his ability to be helpful in the current crisis.

Since it is best not to be at cross-purposes with the hospital personnel, the analyst should clear his professional visits with the administration and, as a professional courtesy, with the surgeon and internist on the case. If surgeons are particularly worried about the patient's mental condition, and/or if they have had some experience themselves with psychotherapy, they may have a relatively enlightened view of the therapist's visits. However, surgeons are at times narcissistic and concrete in their thinking, even vis-à-vis other physicians. The analyst's tact and judgment will dictate how much the patient needs to know of whatever interprofessional difficulties, intricacies, politics, and power struggles might arise. For example, the patient may need to understand that while the analyst made every effort to arrange to see him, reality made it impossible. If this problem is anticipated, the patient can make an advance request, thus assuring visiting privileges for the analyst. Awareness of possible postoperative psychological complications is often enough to enlist surgeon's greater cooperation. Fear of having a psychotic patient on his hands will promote a welcoming attitude toward the psychiatrist.

Many people anticipate that they will spend the day before surgery in mortal fear. The analyst should be familiar with preoperative procedures, including sedation, and with the types of anesthesia available. The analyst and patient should urge the surgeon to commit himself concerning the procedures and anesthetics, thus permitting the analyst and patient to anticipate particular anxieties. The anesthesiologist should discuss the choices of anesthesia prior to the surgery. Occasionally, for instance, pre-anesthesia is given rectally; some patients are more upset by this than by the surgery itself. With modern anesthetics, waking up after surgery is not necessarily unpleasant. If possible, it is helpful to have someone familiar in the room when the patient awakens. Waking up in an intensive care unit, disoriented, fatigued, immobilized, possibly in pain, and completely dependent on others, is a frightening experience, even when the patient is prepared for it. The postoperative environment of the ICU should be discussed in detail. Being able to orient himself, the patient is less likely to react with panic as he awakes from anesthesia. At least when the patient returns to his room, someone familiar should be there to comfort him. The therapist himself can become the supportive link between the preoperative and postoperative states.

REFERENCE

ROSEN, V. H. Psychiatric problems in general surgery. In L. Bellak (Ed.), *Psychology of Physical Illness.* New York: Grune & Stratton, 1952.

21. Experiences of Violence (Mugging, Rape, Accidents)

RAPE

Whether there is a real increase in the incidence of rape or whether the climate of the times simply leads to more frequent reporting of it is unclear. The fact remains that the problems of rape have aroused increasing professional interest.

Rape is now seen primarily as a crime of violence, not primarily an act of a sexual nature. The women's liberation movement has been responsible for this broader understanding of rape. It has become clear that provocativeness on the part of the woman does not usually play a role in rape; most rapists attack the next woman coming their way, apparently almost independent of age or of looks. On the other hand, the prevailing spirit of woman's liberation makes it most difficult to discuss the fact that in some social situations, where the rape victim is not simply assaulted in a dark park, unconscious seductiveness on the part of the woman or poor judgment, possibly combined with unconscious impulses, may still play a role.

When it seems that the woman may have been seductive, it is very important to explore the specific psychodynamics of a woman patient who has been victimized. As with all *major* contemporary events, the impact of the experience has to be seen in relation to the patient's total personality and life history, and common denominators should be established and worked through. Special attention must be paid to masochistic character features and inappropriate guilt feelings related to possible masochistic enjoyment of the violence. Previously existing rape fantasies especially must be explored.

Generally, rape will induce feelings of violation, feelings of helplessness and panic in direct relation to the individual history. Early childhood situations—seduction, forced sex play, primal scenes—will be reawakened with marked intensity.

Management

The Rape Victim, by Elaine Hilberman (1976), explores the socio-cultural context of rape and delineates advances made in helping the rape victim. Reactions to rape are grouped into four phases:

1) *An anticipatory or "threat" phase* describes the fine balance between the need to protect one's illusion of invulnerability and the awareness of the threatening reality, with some attempt to protect oneself from—and prepare oneself for—the danger.
2) The *impact phase* brings increased vigilance as a defense mechanism, followed by diminished alertness, numbness, dullness, and affective and memory disturbances, and a general disorganization. In rape victims studied, 25 percent appeared unperturbed. Twenty-five percent had paralyzing anxiety, hysteria, and confusion. The reamining majority were simply stunned and bewildered.
3) In the *recoil phase,* there is a return of emotional expression and awareness. It is in this phase that the therapist can be particularly useful in helping the patient reconstitute. Depending on how the patient perceives the events, behaviors, and feelings, there will be either a sharp decrease in self-esteem and self-confidence with attendant psychodynamic sequelae, or an adaptive increase in these factors.
4) In the *post-traumatic phase,* the patient has maximally reconstituted and can recall the event, repairing whatever temporary damage was done.

Unresolved, unworked-through sequelae of rape may present as symptoms like claustrophobia, social withdrawal, anxiety attacks, nightmares, and rages loosely focused around issues of helplessness and personal violation.

Supporting the patient in deciding whether to tell the family, the husband or lover, friends or children, and in assessing the implications of not doing so, is an important task for the therapist. For instance, a woman whose "macho" husband was very likely to hold the rape against her, and to see her as devalued, felt unable to tell him about this act of violence. She then acted out violently at her workplace, where the events occurred. She was painfully conflicted in a realistically difficult situation. Concerns about newspaper publicity, community gossip, social and professional ostracism need to be realistically and supportively addressed. Possible pregnancy, venereal disease, the question of legal prosecution of the rapist and dangers of vengeance for reporting the rape are fears that routinely appear and should be explored and resolved.

MUGGING AND BURGLARY

Anamnesis and Assessment

Five houses were burglarized in my neighborhood under similar circumstances. One neighbor who has in general a good adaptation to life did not feel personally threatened and dealt appropriately with the incident. Another neighbor talked of it frequently. He elaborated a distinct fantasy in which he sets a trap for the next intruder. The burglar falls through a trapdoor and is impaled on spikes. This neighbor in his real life is an assertive, aggressive, extremely effective businessman. This burglary, this violation, was felt by him as a real threat to his masculinity. Accustomed to warding off passivity with aggression, he elaborated fantasies in which he pierced the opponent.

The individual's personality will determine the degree of impact and the nature of response to traumatic events. The more fear of passivity, the greater the effect of mugging, burglary, and other such violent crimes. Incidentally, however, some persons are pathologically unconflicted about passivity. One patient enjoyed various acts of "courage." He had enjoyed death-defying war experiences. He frequently shut off the motor when flying his plane and used it as a glider. The same patient was remarkably and genuinely unafraid of a gangster with whom he became involved. Passive in many respects, he was bisexual and his lack of "masculine protest" or macho spirit may have been responsible for the fact that passivity posed almost no threat to him.

Issues of self-esteem are much more likely to appear in men involved in such crimes than in women. Culturally, men are still expected to be strong, to fight and defend themselves. If a man fails to do so when attacked, as is likely and often wise, he is prone to suffer some depreciation of his self-image. Being vulnerable is usually less threatening to a female in terms of issues of self-esteem.

Finally, "bystanders" to violence are often affected and their problems ought to be considered equally seriously. A patient's roommate was murdered in the apartment they shared. The patient actually found the girl dead. She was very disorganized by the experience, and the upset spread through her entire family. All the therapist can do in such a tragic instance is help the patient work through the experience in terms of his or her own personal psychodynamics, history, and general life situation.

Management

As in the case of sexual assaults, it is a delicate procedure to explore invitations, conscious or unconscious, to crime against the person and property. A patient involves himself, for example, with neighbors who are clearly criminal characters. He attends a social function with them, gets beaten up and robbed. After several episodes of this nature, it is important to point out to him that he is exercising poor judgment. The therapist must work with the defective judgment and whatever factors involving unconscious motivations contribute to it. In other instances, the specific meaning of any violence to a given person, in the light of his personal history, has to be analyzed.

Anamnesis and Assessment

Accidents are often forms of acting-out. It is believed, for instance, that many automobile accidents are suicides or suicide attempts. The therapist must thoroughly explore all the details surrounding the "accident," including especially the patient's thought content and preoccupations before, during, and after the event. Fantasies and dreams will also be helpful in making the assessment.

On the anniversary of a very serious car accident in which he had been involved, a patient had an illuminating dream. The patient's major concern had been about his responsibility for the accident, especially as two of his children were in the car. This issue arose in the analysis as part of discussions of his larger problem of impulse control and his fears of his own aggressive impulses, which he dealt with largely by reaction formation. Clearly he was concerned that he may have let his impulses run away with him. His superego reacted and he felt guilt, even though witnesses could unequivocally establish the reality—that he had been standing still at a stop sign and was struck by the other vehicle. He dreamed of little animals that became large and snapped at him. Fairytale animals, with a German-sounding name like the analyst's, looked like straight, tall cacti. They appeared and came at him through a window, producing much anxiety in the dream.

Understanding animals and plants which relate to erectile tissues and phallic strivings , it was evident that the patient experienced the car smashing into him as a phallic attack, with added transference features. In that context, he was also afraid that his own phallus did and could get out of control. Associations to this dream revealed concerns about castration and notions of the vagina as an open wound. To be spared this anxiety, he also had fantasies of being better off as a girl; these were not homosexual wishes per se, but rather the wish to be female represented a means of avoiding fears of the consequences of aggressive masculinity. The car accident was a special precipitating event which kindled specific dynamics—

namely, somebody's phallus getting him or his getting someone else —and the superego reaction to that, resulting in guilt. In addition, transference aspects appear in the similar sounding names shared by the "animals" and the therapist. This example demonstrates the layers of understanding and meaning which may be involved in such "accidental" events—the manifest realities of the accident, the salient aspects of the personality and defenses involved, and the nature of the transference forces.

Management

In order to avoid phenomena akin to traumatic neuroses, to avoid lingering after-effects, denial must be staunchly interpreted. As in pathological mourning or the absence of mourning, the therapist must help the patient do the working-through. Lindemann (1944) found in his classic study of the Boston Coconut Grove fire that surviving victims and relatives have a high incidence of psychosomatic disorders and strictly psychological/psychiatric disorders *if* mourning work is not done. Victims of violent crimes and experiences suffer similarly and an adequate and thorough working-through is crucial.

REFERENCES

HILBERMAN, E. *The Rape Victim.* Washington, D.C.: American Psychiatric Association, 1976.
LINDEMANN, E. Symptomatology and management of acute grief. *Am J. Psychiat.,* 101: 141-148, 1944.

22. Pregnancy and Abortion

If pregnancy occurs in the course of psychotherapy, it is often the analyst's job to educate the patient in detail regarding the anatomical, physiological, and psychological aspects of pregnancy, especially when the obstetrician has not taken the time to discuss these issues thoroughly. Surprisingly, many people still have uncertain and confused concepts of the various aspects of pregnancy and the choices and obligations of parenthood.

Myths and fantasies about pregnancy are very old. The biblical story of the forbidden fruit can be interpreted as a form of symbolic sexuality: the "snake" causes trouble and the apple caught in Adam's throat is a disguised pregnancy. Globus hystericus, the feeling that there is a ball-like object stuck in the throat, is sometimes seen as an hysterical symbolization of the fear of pregnancy, engendered by childhood notions that pregnancy occurs via the mouth. Anorexia is at times related to such fantasies. This concept is often supported by children's statements that the "baby is in the stomach" or the colloquial expression "she has a big stomach." Such childhood fantasies are unconsciously revived by pregnancy.

An unwanted pregnancy, the decisions and their repercussions in keeping or terminating a pregnancy may produce problems and veritable crises, depending on the individual's ego strengths and a variety of other important factors. Although enlightened legislation has minimized or eliminated many realistic obstacles to termination of pregnancy, others remain. Providing possibilities, such as abortion centers, is a necessary provision but not sufficient in terms of dealing with the total problem of an unwanted child.

PREGNANCY

Anamnesis and Assessment

Problematical notions of pregnancy have greatly abated since the advent of enlightened school programs and educational television. But disturbing and overtly pathological reactions are still abundant. Above all, pregnancy is likely to bring out many ambivalences, primarily toward the father of the child. Ambivalence toward a future offspring is frequently an outgrowth of the woman's perceptions of her child being distorted by feelings toward her siblings, particularly younger siblings, and identifications of the future child with the rivaled sibling. One patient had anniversary depressions each time her daughter had a birthday. During pregnancy and after the birth of the child, a close interrelationship of ambivalent feelings existed toward her own mother, her younger sister, and her child.

The sex of the child often produces much fantasy material and conflict. In the course of analytic treatment, a pregnant woman may develop a marked ambivalence toward herself as a woman. This sentiment may then be manifested as hostility toward the unborn child. A patient reported that if she gave birth to a son, she would kill him. Some women will declare with equal vehemence that they want *only* sons, and giving birth to a boy will produce an otherwise unaccountable euphoria. In these latter cases, careful analysis, for example, of such a woman's dreams, may show that this euphoria results from an identification with the male and feelings that she has finally acquired a penis by this circuitous route.

One patient had resisted becoming pregnant for years, creating a problem in her marriage. Analysis showed that a child was perceived not simply as a rival for the husband's affections, but as another presence usurping time and attention. Her narcissism was also manifest in her deep concerns about the effect of pregnancy on her body and her self-image. When she did become pregnant, she developed claustrophobia, intricately related to the idea that the child would be a "burden," a restraint, and keep her from leaving the house.

In extreme forms pregnancy may be experienced as an invasion by the fetus, with destruction of the body. There is a feeling of being parasitized, that the inside of the body is imposing on the outside.

Fear of childbirth itself is less prevalent now because of more enlightened attitudes and wider use of natural childbirth methods, but it may need to be considered in assessing a problematical adjustment to pregnancy. Most younger obstetricians will discuss these new methods with their patients in detail. Fathers frequently participate in the preparation for childbirth and in the delivery itself and, in addition, play an extensively expanded role after birth, making the whole process healthier and less frightening for both parents and probably the child as well.

There are also conscious considerations to be kept in mind regarding pregnancy. Some couples have children in an attempt to hold onto a marriage. Worse still, in a warring relationship, the child often becomes the object through which the parents fight each other. Conversely, one patient who had reason to believe that she could not get pregnant suffered considerable disruption in her marriage when she unexpectedly discovered she was. Her husband, an older man, was not prepared to raise a child. She herself, well set on a professional course, had to reevaluate her life goals. Many conflicts came into sharp focus and produced significant psychological turmoil.

In very young women, pregnancy produces particular problems if the marriage was a carefree love affair with no particular burdens upon it. For the woman, pregnancy and child care often become issues that define her role. Whichever choice is made, a "loss" may be involved. Part of the analyst's job is to help the patient work this through, enabling her to see that she has many choices within the definitions she has given her life. Many women patients work on this problem for a long time. Currently, consciousness-raising groups have been positive forces in the exploration of identity and goals for modern women.

Pregnancy and childbirth are often treated by the media as something negative, even demonic, in which the woman is an unwilling and unsuspecting accomplice. The films "Rosemary's Baby" and "The Omen" are examples. Indeed, women will sometimes feel that the coming child plays such a role, that pregnancy can become the seal of doom, especially for the woman in a bad marriage. This conceptualization often leads to the perception of the child as a malevolent force. A patient whose grown daughter is psychotic had this perception. The daughter's psychosis is related to the mother's attitude since birth, which produced tremendous and constant warfare between them over the years. Now, the legalization of abortion has drastically altered the sealing of such fates. It offers crucial and redeeming options and choices.

Management

Preparation for childbirth, in general terms, would follow strategies and tactics discussed in Chapter 19 regarding preparation for surgery. Specifically, whether it is conscious or not, the fear of childbirth often exists on a deep and primitive level. From an early age women have been told of the pain and suffering of childbirth by their mothers, aunts and others. Many women have had a traumatic experience with a previous childbirth. The analyst must treat the patient's pregnancy and childbirth as a medical event. He must be educational and supportive, exploring all approaches and resources available to the patient, and help make the most appropriate choices for that particular patient. Many women will require help in negotiating the changes in body image, especially in relation to sexuality. Over the past decade, however, many more women have become very sophisticated about these issues. One should not assume, however, that these areas have been sufficiently thought through and they ought to be gently explored.

Postpartum depressions remain a most common complication. The causes are not entirely clear. At times strictly endocrine and metabolic factors seem to play a considerable role. During pregnancy the metabolism is greatly speeded up in general, along with the significant endocrine changes more directly related to the pregnancy itself. Sometimes depression appears to be simply the down side of the metabolic curve. But dynamically, delivery is often seen as a loss, as giving up something that was part of the self, and the woman mourns the lost part. Again, ambivalent feelings toward the child from many sources, as discussed above, colliding with a strong superego, produce the basic dynamics for a depression.

Some postpartum depressions suggest other organic factors. Such depressions occur more frequently after the birth of a male. Androgen levels, which rise considerably during the third trimester, fall after delivery and may produce depression. Similarly, particular patients who suffer from eclampsia, a toxic state which occurs occasionally in pregnant women, are likely to have some residual depression which often resolves as soon as the toxic state subsides. Clearly, however, psychogenic factors can be easily and reasonably woven into these situations, and both the physical and the psychological ought to be rigorously explored and addressed, as indicated.

A specific surgical element, unique to childbirth, and a source of many anxieties and fantasies in women, is the episiotomy, the surgical incision of the vulva. This incision is in reality barely felt because of anesthesia or because at the time of birth the area is so stretched as to be mechanically anesthetized. Repair is usually perfect. It can, in fact, improve the pre-pregnant state of the vagina, if, for example, the vagina were excessively loose due to prior childbirth, congenital or other reasons. Exploration, education, and reassurance are often needed here to offer the woman emotional support in this very sensitive area.

Finally, the effects of pregnancy and childbirth on the prospective father ought to be explored. "Sympathetic" pregnancy, a fear of pregnancy and the dependence and passivity it implies, and many other varied reactions occur. Narcissistic conflicts may be stimulated if the man perceives the coming child as a rival. If it represents a sibling, ambivalence is likely to flare up. The birth of a girl may call forth fantasies anticipating a seductive or overly libidinized relationship. Exploration, education, and support will enable the therapist who has anticipated all possibilities to plan and maximize the benefit to the patient, both male and female, of this major life event.

ABORTION

Anamnesis and Assessment

Despite considerable discussion and controversy in recent years about pregnancy and abortion, a surprising number of women are uninformed about crucial areas involving conception, birth or termination of a pregnancy. The therapist's first concern with a woman in crisis over an unwanted pregnancy is her history in relation to pregnancy, wanted or unwanted. The therapist should determine the cultural milieu in which the patient is functioning, as well as her understanding of the pregnancy in terms of her life situation and the alternatives available to her. The therapist should learn what supportive persons in the woman's life may be called upon. A vivid picture of how the patient felt when she first learned she was pregnant and how she is coping with it is essential. This information will enable the therapist to help the patient take the most appropriate course of action.

A woman struggling with the problem of an unwanted pregnancy and considering an abortion is often caught in confusing crosscurrents of feelings. Conflicts about abortion itself will get in the way of a woman's ability to recognize her own feelings about the pregnancy. Strong feelings, love or hatred, can obscure real feelings and perceptions of what is in her own best interest. For example, clarifying feelings toward the prospective father in the light of the patient's own history in relation to men lessens the possibility that the woman will carry the fetus to term as a romantic notion, or terminate the pregnancy for pathological reasons. The therapist should attempt to determine whether the pregnancy is an acting-out of some unconscious drive or unfulfilled need. Hostility and moral censure from family, friends, and even medical personnel threaten self-esteem and add to the chaos of feelings. The decision to terminate a pregnancy may often be made by a woman despite her religious or moral tenets against such action. If all factors have been properly evaluated and the patient is otherwise comfortable with her decision, this dichotomy is not usually a problem.

A late or delayed termination, in the second or third trimester, presents greater physical and emotional difficulties. Such late decisions are indicative of problems that are not likely to be adequately resolved by the termination of pregnancy. Indeed, the very difficulties and complications inherent in late termination may be perceived as retribution for transgressions. Early evaluation and referral are essential for both medical and psychological well-being.

The legalization of abortion has greatly improved the overall situation. Fears of damage to the woman's body and the image of abortion as a violent, rape-like attack are diminished, though these concerns may still appear symbolically in fantasies and dreams. However, psychodynamic factors are not always lurking, ominous spectres. Many women have abortions with a minimum of psychological complications. Abortion in the early stages of pregnancy need not be physically traumatic and does not require a truly surgical intervention (junction), making it much less of a problem, realistically and psychologically.

Women in their thirties who have no other children usually have the most difficult decision regarding abortion. There is painful anxiety about possibly losing a "last chance." Mothers of young women considering abortion may become ambivalent for a time about the daughter's decision, reminded perhaps that they could have terminated any one of their own pregnancies. Such a woman may even have had abortion in mind when she conceived that same daughter or other children.

Unmarried 14- or 15-year-old girls who become pregnant may want to keep their child, motivated by narcissistic identification, treating the child the way they wish they had been treated. The child takes the place of a doll, and regrettably, in reality, is most often mistreated because of the girl's identification with the "bad mother," mistreating the child as she was mistreated. Adolescent mothers frequently soon lose interest in their child.

Even if the decision to terminate has been carefully weighed, in terms of the pros and cons, the patient may nevertheless display some feelings of despondency after the abortion. This response is natural and possibly even physiological. In cases where there is no such response, the therapist should look for feelings and attitudes which were unresolved prior to the decision to terminate the pregnancy. A history of psychopathology, concomitant medical illness, or medical complications resulting from the abortion usually contribute to the post-abortion response. Suicide, however, is a rare occurrence.

A woman's decision to bear a child and give it up for adoption is often the result of the conscious acceptance of the pregnancy. Many women who decide to have the child, though they know they will give it up, see pregnancy and childbirth as a positive personal experience, and abortion as alien. If the woman is strong enough to go against societal norms (as is usually the case with the unmarried woman) and have the child, she is also usually realistic about the problems of raising a child alone and is sometimes able to give the child up for adoption without severe crisis. However, she may depend on the therapist to either redefine or affirm the factors she has considered in reaching her decision.

Accidental pregnancy by definition precludes any real planning beyond the decision to continue the pregnancy or not. The problems of rearing and maintaining a child are often obscured by the anticipated emotional benefits of motherhood. The patient should be helped to recognize and to begin planning for major changes in her life situation if she decides to bear a child. More important than the realities of the woman's age and economic status are the reasons and attitudes behind the decision to continue the pregnancy. The therapist should explore the expectations in continuing *this* pregnancy versus the motivations to bear and raise any child or children.

Management

The therapist's role is *not* that of the patient's counselor. He should act as an educator and guide, laying out all the options, enabling the woman to make a decision that weighs all factors and is best for her life circumstances. She is likely to be influenced by existing cultural and religious factors, as well as by her family and friends. These forces often cause conflict and anxiety, but once a decision is made—one in which the woman has participated and with which she feels comfortable—she will benefit greatly in terms of her personal growth.

To this end the therapist should educate the patient regarding all aspects of birth control and family planning to better help avoid the misfortune of another unwanted pregnancy in a woman's life. For the younger woman, compatible contraceptive techniques should be explored. In cases of recurring pregnancies which are all terminated, in which it appears that the woman considers abortion a viable form of birth control, more realistic alternatives should be stressed. For the stable woman who wants no more children, tubal ligation may be a logical decision and need not create any real problem. Analyzing the "decision" to have or not have children is a good instance of preventive mental health work. Educating prospective parents, helping them explore their feelings and understand children in different phases of growth, and screening for pathology, will benefit the parent, the child, and our complex society as well. Almost anyone can become a parent. A great deal of education and suitability should be prerequisites for parenthood, and in that respect abortion, family planning, and parenthood support systems are a rich potential means of genuine preventive medicine which can promote mental health.

23. Financial Reverses
and Job Loss

A careful financial assessment of a patient's ability to afford analytic or psychotherapeutic treatment before entering it is essential. Unrealistic plans will only cause harm to the patient, the treatment, and the therapist. Sometimes, patients are really not aware either of how well-off they are, or how poor they are, this often being subject to denial.

Part of the anamnesis should be an evaluation of the general financial life situation. An individual may indeed have a very modest income from his or her work, but have a large endowment or trust fund. Someone else may have a large income but such great expenses that any sizeable fee would nevertheless cause serious problems. Above all, some budgeting has to be done, taking into consideration the anticipated length of the treatment. There is no point in starting treatment only to have it interrupted because the patient cannot afford to continue, or the therapist cannot afford not to be paid.

Of course, there are certain situations where all therapists will, if they are in a position to do so, either decrease their customary fee or make some arrangement with the patient for deferred payment. Such an arrangement can cause both realistic and transference difficulties, and these difficulties must be anticipated and planned for. As far as reality is concerned, some definite dates for repayment should be set, and the rate of repayment established. Such arrangements are often necessary, particularly with analytic candidates or other professionals who are starting out on their careers. While any senior person might take on a young colleague at a reduced fee, this becomes impossible if the practice of a senior person consists mostly of young trainees.

As to the transference complications, it is obvious that a favorable arrangement may induce feelings of dependence, some oral gratifications, and even some resistances, which need to be analyzed in the course of the treatment.

As with other extrinsic circumstances, financial reverses occurring throughout or during the treatment process often can *not* be anticipated. A person may lose a job, have heavy losses in his business or investments, or have unexpected drains of his assets. Provisions have to be made for such occurrences. The arrangements will depend on the nature of the patient and the circumstances. In some cases it is indeed better to at least interrupt treatment, after suitable working-through of the problem, until a later date when the patient can afford to begin treatment again. In other situations, the patient's personality and the therapist's assets may permit them to go through a period of decreased payments or no payment at all, with the idea of later compensation.

All other things being equal, it is best in such a case that the patient take a loan and pay his fee out of the loan, thus avoiding the transference complications, as well as the realistic complications for the analyst. At times, I have found it fair to make myself responsible for the interest accumulated on the cost of the loan for the advantage of not having to wait for payment and to help avoid possible transference complications.

In specific situations, like divorce, legal arrangements can be made so that the divorced couple's obligations to one another are clear. Usually it is the woman who is at least somewhat financially dependent after a divorce, and the therapist should help her assure that the ex-husband provides adequately for her therapy. This helps prevent one party from exercising his displeasure by withholding funds.

Similarly, a difficult situation exists when parents pay for treatment of adolescents or young adults. In effect they are then in charge of the treatment. The analyst can predict that as part of the process, especially with overly compliant young persons, the patient is going to want to rebel and be independent. Not all parents will appreciate this "therapeutic" change, and will sometimes feel that the treatment has made the patient more of a problem. If circumstances permit, it is wise that money be set aside, preferably in escrow, against which therapy bills can be drawn. Otherwise, patient and therapist will be essentially at the parents' whim and mercy.

Job Loss is a frequent threat and traumatic occurrence in the lives of many people. When it occurs in the course of psychoanalysis or psychotherapy, it may be a direct, realistic threat to the continuation of treatment, as well as a difficult psychological reality. Such an event involves far more than a financial threat. In our culture, a person is largely defined by the job he holds. A job means a certain role, a certain place in a hierarchy. A job provides a clearly defined structure, which most people need. We need a place to go in the morning, a place to leave at night, and specific tasks to perform. Without structure, many people feel hopelessly lost. Most jobs, within their context, support significant aspects of self-esteem. Other aspects of self-esteem and role are further supported by a job in relation to a patient's family and friends. The "pater familias" who is accustomed to bringing home the bacon finds himself seriously and broadly threatened by a job loss.

By virtue of being a loss, job loss can be understood in terms of the dynamics of depression. A realistic loss is experienced as a loss of love. The person who is responsible for the patient's loss is usually the recipient of aggressive feelings. As in a depression, the contemporary figure may also stand for a figure from the patient's past, so that job loss represents an historical loss. The greater the problem with self-esteem that existed prior to job loss, the more severe the reaction to the loss is likely to be. The feeling of being deceived, dynamically speaking, by a love object is likely to lead to rage or depressive equivalents such as fatigue, sleeplessness, loss of appetite, or overeating.

The secondary gain of passivity also has to be kept in mind. Passivity, the absence of responsibility, may soon come to be felt as pleasant by a patient and make treatment all the more difficult. This is especially true if unemployment insurance or other resources make the reality situation less than dire. Such "insurance neurosis" is not merely undesirable from a moralistic standpoint, but has additional ill-effects on the person's self-esteem, even though a part of him enjoys the enforced passivity and regressive tendencies.

Finally, transference manifestations of job loss are likely to appear in the course of therapy. Since the patient feels increased helplessness, dependency may come more to the fore. Rage over the loss, the feeling of disappointment or deception may enter into the transference. The realistic loss may be misused for acting-out in a variety of ways.

MANAGEMENT

Under no circumstances should the patient be permitted to interrupt treatment in the urgent immediacy of the first panic. It is the therapist's primary task to see that all the realistic aspects of the situation are properly considered. In some instances, for example, the patient's salary may continue for some time; a long due notice may be given. In effect, no real immediate change in the patient's life occurs and therapy can be continued. In other cases, the general financial resources of the reasonably well-off patient should be considered; for the less well endowed, unemployment insurance, social security, etc. should be explored.

If circumstances are indeed dire, the therapist may wish to extend himself as much as his circumstances permit, arranging for payment at some future date. Treatment under such circumstances may only be extended for the time period necessary to help the patient deal with his realistic problems in relation to his job loss and work through psychodynamic ones. Then it may be necessary to interrupt treatment until the patient can afford to return. In such instances there are two major variables to be considered: The therapist's financial status must be considered in establishing a time limit, albeit a variable one, for treatment on a deferred payment basis; and the patient's capacity to tolerate incurring a debt and possibly bearing gratitude must be explored, along with the host of usual transference problems.

While one has to pay attention first to the realistic aspects, these realistic aspects and subjective meaning will frequently merge. Only after due appreciation of the realistic details, however, is the patient likely to be willing to enter into the general and then the specific meanings that the job loss has for him at this particular point in his life. It is important for the therapist to take an active role in planning, reality-testing, and assessing the future with the patient. Additionally, in order to avoid depressive features, which might interfere with initiative in these tasks, antidepressant medication may be indicated.

24. Divorce

Divorce, *before* entering treatment, at *the time* of entering treatment, or in the *course* of treatment, has become an extremely frequent occurrence and is still on the increase. It presents a special problem to psychoanalysis and psychotherapy. The rule that patients should not make major decisions while in psychoanalysis or psychotherapy should, if at all possible, be applied. However, the temper of the times dictates greater flexibility. The increased speed and mobility of our world affect the readiness with which people make decisions, exercise options, and pursue alternatives, with or without analysis or therapy. While it is best to adhere to the rule of "no major decisions while in dynamic turmoil due to therapeutic changes," if there is indication that the "decision" is being motivated by irrational conflicts or displaced transference feelings stirred up in the course of analysis, such a life change should obviously be delayed until the motivation is clear.

The decision to divorce may often be a special situation. A woman in her mid-thirties who is in a bad marriage and concerned about passing her child-bearing years understandably has mixed feelings about waiting three to five years to the end of her analysis to make a decision about divorce. A patient who enters treatment with an equivocal decision to divorce must be distinguished from the one who decides to divorce in the course of treatment and the one who decides to go into treatment *after* divorce. Both these latter situations present definite psychodynamic problems and indicate the need for rigorous assessment.

Divorce appears in three phenomenologically distinguishable types:

1) The *extended divorce*—there is much fluctuation and indecision but divorce appears to be inevitable in the long run. The couple may have attempted to live apart at least once and one partner wants the divorce more than the other.

2) The *developmental* crisis divorce—the nexus of the relationship has changed, along with each partner's self-image. This often occurs in mid-life. The children leave home, the wife and/or husband experience a shift in role or have a psychological or physiological "change of life," often precipitated by an operation such as a hysterectomy or prostatectomy.

3) The *impulsive gesture* divorce—most common in younger marriages which are very stormy. Divorce is precipitous and violent.

ANAMNESIS AND ASSESSMENT

Very little has been written about why people marry and why they marry each other, what specific dynamics and circumstances are pertinent, necessary and sufficient. Certain patterns, however, seem evident and are repetitive.

Two people who have lived together happily for years, unmarried, may, under the enigmatic pressures of a marriage bond, fight day and night. Sometimes the man becomes impotent or the woman frigid. The marriage bond has taken on the forbidden oedipal aspect which is real enough to disturb the relationship. Very often the first marriage is more burdened by oedipal implications and other childhood dynamics. Many people are able to have a much more mature relationship the second time around. Older and more mature, they are able to choose a spouse who is less confused in their own mind with the image of the parent or the parent antithesis (the antithetical object choice occurs when the parent is such a forbidden figure that the spouse must have *no* similarity to the parent in facial features, character structure, ethnic background or religious affiliation).

The remarkably narcissistic individual often finds a spouse he can relate to on the basis of mutual narcissism. The marriage contract is an agreement to continue to live narcissistic lives. If the marriage becomes disturbed and divorce occurs, a heightened narcissism ensues, with a residual inability to develop social relationships again. This patient will present a major therapeutic problem. He will have great difficulty with object relations and should be treated with great caution as regards his marital situation. The therapist should do all that is possible and appropriate to avoid having the patient rush into a divorce because he will usually be unable to find a suitable partner again unless the therapist is able to work successfully with the narcissism, which is usually a very difficult problem.

For some patients, divorce may symbolize not only separation but desertion, and may play a significant role in the evolution of a major depression. A specific patient, for example, spent years in a residential therapeutic community after being orphaned early in life. Furthermore, his history revealed that he was plagued by a number of other "desertions" in his childhood. He experienced his wife's request for a divorce as another catastrophic desertion. It should be noted that even without such a history of abandonment, divorce takes on this meaning generally, to a greater or lesser extent.

People with "phobic" attitudes toward other people arrange marriage patterns that facilitate dilution of the marital relationship. It is amazing, but not unusual, to find a couple who have been married for decades, where the husband is away all week nearly every week of the year and the pair spend only an occasional weekend together. The husband spends the weekend playing golf or tennis; the wife visits relatives or friends. The therapist might feel this is clearly reason enough for divorce, but a careful history will reveal that all the patient's relationships have had a similar quality. In therapy, no transference relationship is allowed to develop. Everyone is kept at a distance, for myriad reasons. In one case, a patient had a very intense relationship with his mother. As he grew older, he felt deserted and disappointed by her. He developed such a fear of involvement with anyone else who might so painfully disappoint him that he arranged to have relationships with very little emotional involvement. Many people arrange to find a comfortable distance from each other. The patient who keeps people at great distances has made an unconscious choice which the therapist must first recognize. No other type of relationship will be bearable unless the unconscious motivation is first thoroughly analyzed.

Perhaps the most pernicious of patterns frequently seen is the sadomasochistic relationship. To some extent this kind of relatedness plays a part in many marriages, but where it is fundamental, it presents a particularly difficult therapeutic problem. Such people have talked about divorce, sometimes for decades. However, they really do *not* want a therapist to interfere with the marital relationship and the therapist must be sure to fully appreciate the libidinization involved in the violence each does to or receives from the other. Even in divorce, usually a particularly nasty affair, they will continue a similar relatedness to each other and with others. If the analyst or therapist allows himself to get drawn into this kind of situation, both partners will direct negative feelings toward him as being the one at fault. He then becomes a part of the sadomasochistic network. This kind of situation is particularly difficult to handle, even for the most skilled and experienced clinician.

MANAGEMENT

The therapist must, above all, give himself and the patient enough time to understand the dynamics of the relationship to the spouse and the specific dynamics involved in the decision to divorce. Very frequently, the marital relationship is only one particular example of the patient's difficulties in object relationships. The patient and analyst should try to work through such difficulties in therapy without the patient necessarily making a decision to divorce. Sometimes it appears that problems of object relations in both spouses are so serious and irreversible that, rather than divorce, it is better for the people concerned to remain in their relatively poor marriage and to try to improve whatever aspects they can. In some cases, the marital problems cloud the general pathology and the therapist becomes fully aware of the degree of the pathology of the patient's object relations only after a divorce has taken place.

Value judgments are unavoidable in the course of psychoanalysis and psychotherapy. But the therapist should try to minimize value judgments in all situations, including divorce situations. Certainly it is hard to avoid such judgments, since even remaining silent may express a value judgment. It is almost impossible for a therapist to remain consistently neutral. Especially in certain situations, like the sadomasochistic marital relationship, it is imperative to remain within the interpretive role. If both partners are in treatment, even consultation with the therapist of the other spouse is fraught with the danger of arousing more suspicion and affecting the therapist's own neutrality, though he gains a clearer understanding of the spouse's situation.

The more severely disturbed the judgment of the patient, however, the more reason the therapist has to enter in as an auxiliary ego. If the patient in a sadomasochistic marriage, for example, is psychotic, the therapist should do the reality testing and, if necessary, involve other people to protect the patient. If the patient is primarily a neurotic personality, the actual intervention should be primarily interpretation rather than participation. The therapist's decision rests primarily on the degree of the patient's pathology. If the therapist enters in as actively as he might like to, it is likely to lead eventually to negative transference and the patient's departure from treatment. Only if the situation demands it should the therapist enter in actively and set limits.

If the therapist *must* enter in, it is best to follow the procedures of interpretation and management discussed for acting-out. As in the acting-out situation where the patient is acting in a self-destructive way, the therapist can define the limits of acceptability. In such cases, reality testing is the function the therapist is engaged in most.

Ideally, circumstances permitting, both spouses should go into treatment together. If the couple contemplating divorce can be convinced to wait, the result will be better, especially in working out relationships with other people afterwards. People trying to establish new relationships after a divorce or separation often get into great difficulty, reflecting the nature of their overall difficulties in object relations. Following a divorce, the therapist can help the patient learn from a series of object relationships. These relationships may well all share a common denominator which, when recognized, can provide the patient with powerful insight into the nature of his or her own interactions with others.

Many mental health workers try to perform marriage counseling with the intent of keeping the marriage together when, realistically, they should be preparing the couple for divorce. The tenuousness of some marital situations should become apparent in a few sessions, especially if both partners are present. It is important for the therapist to help the couple face their decision by talking frankly about the issues. If only one partner wants a divorce, the therapist can help avoid one partner's manipulation of the other by inviting both for at least one joint session. By so doing, the therapist also lessens the possibility of his own value judgments influencing the situation. Even having the whole family present will clarify the problems that have been shared with the various members. An imminent divorce discussed and shared by the family can help expedite the process of separation in a less traumatic manner. There need be no age restriction. Even a young child can be enlightening regarding his parents' marital problems. Each partner's lawyer may also be present if possible during the family session or sessions to observe the family interaction.

Specifically, when divorce arises as a special problem or crisis in psychoanalysis or psychotherapy, the following measures are crucial:

1) Deal with any suicidal or homicidal risk engendered by the situation.
2) Identify the events that led to the decision to divorce, help the couple find out what went wrong, and "build a fence" around the trouble. There are civilized and uncivilized ways to go through a divorce and isolating the trouble helps give the couple perspective about each other and discourages the danger of excessive discomfort and reprisal.
3) It is important to discuss basic arrangements for the dependent spouse and children.
4) The therapist should help each partner cope with the new

situation, fear of living alone, and anxiety about being separated from the children. Sadness, remorse, and rage concerning the past or the new situation are common. The therapist must help each partner reconstitute a sense of mastery to alleviate feelings of being overwhelmed.

5) A part of therapy will be to consolidate the new stability, to discuss feelings about a sense of loss, and systematically explore and develop a broad base for new life situations.

Parenthetically, for patients in treatment who are involved in divorce, paradoxically, it may be best to keep a minimum of notes or other material that could be subpoenaed and used against a patient. Adversarial court procedures do not inspire confidence or tolerate professional judgment.

25. Third-Party Involvement

It is a fact of our times that, increasingly, third parties are involved in the psychotherapeutic situation. There were always occasions when a parent or spouse paid for treatment and thus entered the psychotherapeutic relationship. More recently, insurance carriers, including Medicaid and Medicare, have played this role. Currently, the concept of peer review and PSRO has come into greater consideration and has introduced its own third parties into the psychotherapeutic process.

ANAMNESIS AND ASSESSMENT

Of all the difficulties created by third-party involvement, problematic interaction with a parent or spouse is the oldest one. In cases of small children or adolescents, the treatment is essentially at the mercy of the parent's willingness to pay. This situation is usually most sensitive in the treatment of adolescents. These patients may present initially as shy and docile, with obsessions or depressions, but in the course of treatment they gain more freedom and independence. In manifestating this newly gained independence, they are likely to express themselves more openly, especially regarding their parents, and behave more autonomously. Not infrequently, both of these manifestations of progress are poorly appreciated by the parent paying the bill, and he will want to interrupt the treatment. Similar situations often hold true with spouses, especially with the husbands of women in treatment. The woman may initially be submissive and compliant in her marriage. She comes seeking treatment for depression. In the course of analytic treatment, she is likely to experience character changes which may not at all please her husband, whereupon he will complain and want to stop her treatment.

A totally different situation exists with regard to evaluation of treatment for third-party payers such as governmental agencies or insurance companies. A prime requisite for psychotherapy is privacy. The patient must have the feeling that he or she can communicate with the therapist in full confidence and that very personal and intimate matters will not be revealed to others. It is difficult enough if part of that private relationship is invaded by people close to one. It is all the worse if disclosure is made to governmental agencies and other institutions who are likely to record such data in information banks, providing easy access for almost anyone. A similar, though not equally extreme, problem prevails if peer review or PSRO is under consideration.

MANAGEMENT

In cases where the parent, spouse, other significant person is involved as a third party, the solution lies in early preparation. If the potential problems are anticipated, occasional conjoint sessions can be scheduled; if indicated and possible, treatment for the third party may also be arranged. In difficult cases, with adolescents specifically, it may be advisable to ask that money for the treatment be put in escrow in a bank, against which monthly payment may be drawn. This removes the direct control of the financial compensation from the parental "third party" payer who is most likely to interfere.

In evaluating cases for institutional third parties, it is most useful to utilize the system of ego function assessment (see Chapter 2; Bellak, Chassan, Gediman & Hurvich, 1973; Bellak, Hurvich & Gediman, 1973; Bellak & Faithorn, 1978; Ciompi, Agne & Dauwalde, 1976). When asked for a report on a patient, his actual functioning in terms of ego function ratings can be provided. Previous profiles can be compared to recent profiles. In addition, ratings showing *highest* and *lowest* levels of functioning give clearer pictures of where the patient stands now, where specific improvement has taken place, and where additional change is needed. This form of assessment for third parties has several advantages. The criteria are clearly defined. Though technical and part of the whole matrix of psychoanalytic theory, they are readily understandable to an intelligent layman. Functions such as reality testing and judgment are almost obvious, and the others, such as autonomous functioning, can be defined easily. Another advantage lies in the fact that statistical reliability and validity have been established for ego function assessment. It is therefore possible to evaluate a patient for a peer review committtee or for other third parties and get independent-rater validity. Such quantitative statements are far superior to vague verbal statements. Also, the process can be used with much greater confidence and conviction and, very importantly, involves little invasion of privacy. It also decreases the often misleading "labeling" effect of the official diagnostic nomenclature, which may be demanded as part of the report.

REFERENCES

BELLAK, L., CHASSAN, J., GEDIMAN, H., & HURVICH, M. Ego function assessment of analytic psychotherapy combined with drug therapy. *J. Nervous and Mental Dis.,* 158 (6):465-469, 1973.

BELLAK, L. & FAITHORN, P. Weekly Psychiatry Update Series, Lessons 34, 35, and 36 on Ego Function Assessment. Edited by Frederick F. Flach, M.D. P. Biomedia, Inc., 1978.

BELLAK, L., HURVICH, M., & GEDIMAN, H. *Ego Functions in Schizophrenics, Neurotics and Normals.* New York: John Wiley & Sons, 1973.

CIOMPI, L., AGUE, C., & DAUWALDE, J. L'objectivation de changements psychodynamiques: Expériences avec une version simplifiée des "Ego Strength Rating Scales de Bellak, et al." Paper read at the 10th International Congress of Psychotherapy, Paris, July 10, 1976.

26. Bereavement and Threat of Death

DEFINITIONS

Bereavement, as an event in the course of treatment, requires recognition of the fact that a powerful emotional experience has intersected with the therapeutic process. If it should happen to come at a time when the patient is already involved with object loss, the reaction may be especially severe. If the patient is involved with other themes, the therapist must be prepared to abandon whatever issues he and the patient are working on and deal with the bereavement, as is true with any other intercurrent situation. This change of focus may produce a slowing down of the therapeutic process, or it may lead to major progress.

Bereavement as an intercurrent event should call to mind the usual dynamic factors. Freud's classic paper "On Mourning and Melancholia" (1915) and such milestones as Lindemann's paper on the aftermath of the Coconut Grove Fire, published in 1944, and a host of others in the psychoanalytic literature are available to delineate these dynamics in considerable detail. It is important to remember, however, that, as with any stressful intercurrent event, bereavement is likely to highlight both the strengths and the weaknesses in the patient's personality structure, and from this strictly technical standpoint, it can be especially illuminating. If the death involves someone who has lingered on in a long illness, partial mourning and some working-through may have taken place before the actual treatment. Especially in the case of loss of a parent, the patient may emerge from the mourning with greater individuation. In our culture, or at least our past culture, the loss of a father has often lead to a real coming of age for a son, especially if successfully handled in therapy. On the other hand, both the pathological lack of mourning and prolonged mourning which has turned into a pathological process and/or a depression indicate the need for active therapeutic intervention.

The therapist should not actively intervene in the work of mourning as long as the patient himself is performing it. The therapist enters into the dynamics of the bereavement only after some of the acuteness has worn off and the patient seems to need help, and then only at a carefully measured pace. When therapeutic intervention is indicated, the areas requiring exploration include the reaction to object loss, the particular meaning of the object relation of the departed, superego reactions, and feelings of loss, of disappointment, of rage and helplessness.

The treatment of fatally ill patients has developed greatly in recent years, but is still something relatively new. Freud treated Anton von Freund, a man suffering from a fatal malignancy, and apparently succeeded in relieving his anxiety and pain. In gratitude, von Freund provided the initial funding for the International Psychoanalytic Publishing Company. Today there is a large body of literature on the psychological impact of death and the process(es) of dying. While it is not traditionally a major psychoanalytic issue and has been legitimized by other clinical psychiatric or psychotherapeutic subgroups, the analyst should redefine his therapy when the actual death of a patient is imminent or, for that matter, when death threatens one close to the patient, including the analyst himself.

ANAMNESIS AND ASSESSMENT

With impending death, the analyst must primarily ascertain the patient's specific notions about death itself. Death holds an amazing variety of meanings and fears for different individuals. Some people, for example, harbor the fear of being buried alive and suffocating. Others are disgusted by metamorphosed fears of oral aggression and imagine that the worms will eat them. These people often prefer cremation, while cremation for others represents an overwhelming and total loss of identity. Ultimately, separation anxiety, being all alone, is a standard aspect of the fear of death for most people. This anxiety is often accompanied by oral greed and envy that others are going to continue to live while the dying individual is being cheated, deprived. Such specific concerns about death can be exquisitely discrete. One patient, in the face of death, was almost exclusively concerned with lying nude on the marble slab at the undertaker's. The feeling of exposure under these circumstances was particularly unbearable.

Alternatively, the fear of dying is often much greater than the fear of being dead. Dying may be seen as an agony, suffering, possibly with sadomasochistic overtones, while death is a form of rest, of sleep, and of no particular threat. A patient with a fear of flying was exclusively concerned about flights over water. Crashing in the ocean would mean being tortuously devoured by sharks—piecemeal. Another patient with a similar fear was unconcerned about instantaneous death in a plane crash, but rather was terrified of surviving such an accident but finding herself in a remote area and dying from lack of water and food. More conventionally, many patients facing death become preoccupied with their affairs, putting their life, their homes, in order. The "incidental" fact of dying is merely an occasion which threatens one with exposure of oneself as "dirty." Broadly, there is usually fear of the passivity involved in impending death and being dead. The fundamental fears, anxieties and fantasies of patients in these helpless states must be carefully explored.

MANAGEMENT

As mentioned previously, there are at least three forms in which dealing with death may become essential in the course of an analysis:

1) The death threatens the patient himself;
2) The death threatens a significant figure in the patient's life;
3) The death threatens the analyst or therapist himself.

Naturally, there is a certain overlap in all these instances; however, at the same time, distinctly separate features are associated with each circumstance.

In the case where the patient faces the death of a loved one, the feelings, particularly the ambivalent feelings towards that figure, need to be thoroughly but tactfully explored. It is true that the more negative feelings one has about an individual, the more difficult it is to face his or her death. For example, in some instances involving severely obsessive-compulsive patients in late middle-age, who harbor complex feelings of hostility and symbiosis towards their aged parents and who have spent literally years anticipating their reaction to the death of the parent, negative feelings and perhaps even death wishes are bound to exist. This situation is particularly complex when the death of the parents promises considerable financial reward for the patient. It is best to encourage the patient in such a situation to act as much within his conscience as possible, to be what he would consider a conscientious offspring. In some variation, this also holds true for spouses who may have an unconscious, preconscious or conscious expectation of freedom associated with the expectation of death of the mate. At the same time, more traditional sentiments such as rage over being abandoned or complex feelings precipitated by having to care for an ill person in whom death is anticipated are rather routine (Berezin, 1970). In this context, it is important to remember that, with any kind of impending death, the analyst must primarily ascertain the patient's specific notions about death itself, which, as mentioned, vary tremendously in terms of idiosyncratic leanings and fears.

Of course, these fantasies play a particular role in the case of possible impending death of the patient himself or herself. Predictably, denial may play an outstanding role, as well as these highly individualized fantasies of what death may mean. Surprisingly enough, it is often true that the more seriously ill a patient and the closer the impending death, the more easily it is borne. It is as if denial and/or acceptance become much more effective than in the case of the patient who has some vague potential threat.

REFERENCES

BEREZIN, M. A. The psychiatrist and the geriatric patient; Partial grief in family members and others who care for the elderly patient. *Geriatric Psychiatry*, 4:53-64, 1970.

FREUD, S. Mourning and melancholia. In *Collected Papers*. London: Hogarth Press, 1915, Vol. 4.

LINDEMANN, E. Symptomatology and management of acute grief. *Amer. Journal of Psychiat.*, 101:141-148, 1944.

IV. Problems of the Therapist

Alas, psychoanalysts and other therapists are human, for better and for worse, and good and bad things happen to them while they treat others. Since our lives as therapists are so closely interwoven with our patients in transference and countertransference, almost anything that happens to us has some effect on our patients and in turn on our own state and our own relationship to the patient.

In this part a few of the more commonly occurring situations affecting an analyst or therapist's life are discussed. It is part of the burdens of a therapist that some troublesome and even critical conditions have to be borne with the additional concern about their effect on patients. If an analyst breaks his arm, he has not only his fracture to bear, but also the castration anxiety it arouses in some patients!

27. Intercurrent Events: Marriage, Pregnancy, Childbirth, Divorce, Moving, Threatening or Actual Illness, Death

INTRODUCTION

The therapist, one hopes, is a stable figure. Ideally, the sessions should be at the same time, in the same place. The therapist should present himself as a relatively anonymous, untroubled person who originally was thought of in the extreme as a screen or tabula rasa, but who is now more often conceptualized as a reasonably neutral human being. This permits the patient a regression to the transference neurosis in psychoanalysis, and gives the patient a feeling of security in all psychotherapy. I entered the qualifier "ideally" because this state of affairs, though undoubtedly offering many advantages, produces an artifact. Some real life events may bring to the analysis previously unsuspected problems: rage, jealousy, affection, and a large number of anxieties.

In all intercurrent conditions of the therapist, one main rule must be observed, namely that one should attempt to maintain as much therapeutic neutrality as is possible without, however, creating artificial situations or deceptions or failing to respond to and interact with the patient in a reasonable and human way where it is indicated.

If the therapist appears with an arm in a cast, it is only sensible to listen first to the patient's fantasies and general notions about it, but not ignore actual concern and briefly acknowledge, "Yes, I did fracture my arm, but it's well on the way to healing." Anything else is almost like a game, and does not acknowledge the human relationship between patient and therapist. On the other hand, this is no occasion for telling a long story to the patient or seeking his or her sympathy.

If the therapist is or was ill, and the patient makes correct observations, the same basic rule should hold true. One listens, one learns from what the patient has to say, and then in a simple way acknowledges that the patient is right—validates his perceptions—and deals with his response in the usual analytic way.

To deny certain situations is only to further *confuse the patient's reality testing*, instead of helping it. If a therapist has recently been married and the patient notices the new wedding ring, it would be poor technique to let the patient believe that it has been there all along, and that he has just failed to notice it. Again, after maintaining enough silence to permit the patient to express thoughts and fantasies, I believe it is constructive to acknowledge reality and to say, "You are absolutely right—the ring is new, and I was married recently." One can then learn a great deal from the patient's reactions.

Something similar holds true for the therapist who becomes pregnant in the course of a patient's treatment. If the patient does not see anything when she has come to show her pregnancy markedly, it is only appropriate to raise the question as to why the patient has not remarked on it, and one can learn a good deal about denial and related problems. It is certainly only reasonable to acknowledge the pregnancy, if the patient remarks on it—again, giving the patient sufficient chance to fantasize and conjecture.

In all these instances, the problem is one of maintaining a delicate balance between the position of analytic neutrality and the need to deal with realistic human considerations. The analyst should avoid an artificial situation often created by the stone-mask approach, which in turn runs the risk of confusing the patient. Below, a number of frequently occurring conditions are briefly discussed.

MOVING

When an analyst moves, even within a relatively small perimeter, the patient experiences a variety of changes: a different kind of a trip, a different kind of a neighborhood, and above all, a different office. The lack of familiarity often produces some anxiety. Critique of the new office often represents transference feelings. Last, though not least, patients are very acute observers because their perception is sensitized by their transference feelings and they will find many faults which may not be comfortable for the analyst or therapist to hear about. Very frequently, the change in the location will produce dreams which reveal a patient's unconscious reactions to the change.

If the analyst actually changes his location to another city or another state, extensive preparation of the patient is necessary. If possible, the patient should be told at least months in advance, and a termination date set. The patient must be helped to make realistic alternative arrangements. Separation problems must be worked through, and an adequate summary prepared for use by another therapist, should the patient choose to continue with someone else.

As part of the process of separation by moving, general separation anxieties can be very usefully worked through. On the realistic side, the therapist should make sure that the patient will have his forwarding address so that he and/or his future therapist can get in touch, if desirable.

MARRIAGE OF THE THERAPIST

Ordinarily, an analyst/therapist will no more announce his or her marriage than any other aspects of his private life. Patients, however, may become aware of the change of status in a number of ways. One is by hearing about it in some social situation. Another is that they may notice that the therapist is wearing a ring, or the new spouse may become visible to the patient at some time, especially if the offices are adjacent to or part of the home.

If one has good reason to assume that the patient has had occasion to observe the change in status by one means or another, but does not say anything, it will pay to carefully observe dreams, associations, and other reactions. At a suitable point in treatment, the analyst can interpret the fact that the patient apparently has been aware of this change but has not said anything about it. Useful dynamic inferences can usually be drawn under these circumstances.

Whenever a patient finds out about the analyst's marriage, chances are that one may observe a wide range of feelings, including jealousy, rivalry and oedipal problems. These may be reflected in dreams and fantasies, and can indeed be very useful for further understanding of a variety of problems.

If the patient has had *good reason* to become aware of the analyst/therapist's changed status, it would be reasonable for the therapist to make a simple declaration of fact. While we do not share our private lives with our patients voluntarily or unnecessarily, it is erroneous to stay protected behind analytic anonymity (possibly because to do otherwise might be uncomfortable for the analyst). This would create an inordinately artificial situation or further confound the patient, impairing reality testing and judgment. If the analyst does not validate the patient's perception and state the facts plainly and clearly, this might well be experienced as a deception.

PREGNANCY, MOTHERHOOD AND FATHERHOOD

Pregnancy, motherhood and fatherhood are other intercurrent events which often stir up feelings and conflicts in patients. The latter, of course, is usually less noticeable. Observing an increase in abdominal size in the female therapist may reawaken sibling rivalries, produce passive fears in male patients, or evoke envy, jealousy, and identification in patients of both sexes. Pregnancy makes it clear to patients that there is a man in the therapist's life and may produce appropriate conflicts and other complications in response to that fact.

Fatherhood, of course, is not so often brought to the patient's attention. However, if, for example, office and quarters are being shared, conversations or remarks between the psychiatrist and his colleagues may be overheard or some such other situation may arise whereby the patient is made cognizant of the therapist's changed status and the new child in his life. In the case of either male or female therapist, pregnancy fantasies and dreams about pregnancy may provide extremely useful material for analysis and insight.

DIVORCE

In view of the fact that divorce rates are so high, divorce is very likely to occur in an analyst's family or in his own marriage. Again, the patient may hear about it socially, or may become aware of it by a relocation of the therapist's office or other observable changes in the therapist's life. The patient may also correctly perceive tension and upset in the therapist's demeanor. As usual, we analyze as much as possible the notions, fantasies, and dreams of the patient, and preferably only after that, when appropriate, do we announce the concrete facts. This, in turn, will lead to reactions by the patient which may lend themselves to useful analyzing. The patient may reexperience his parents' divorce. He may suddenly see the analyst in a different light, as an available male or female figure or, generally speaking, as a sexual figure and at times as a failure, as a person with poor control of impulses. Frequently, pleasure or disappointment in the plain humanity and fallibility of the therapist is experienced, which may lend itself to valuable reality testing and interpretation.

ACTUAL OR THREATENED INTERCURRENT PHYSICAL ILLNESS IN THE THERAPIST OR ANALYST

If the therapist or analyst has a physical illness that is likely to incapacitate him for any length of time, he must provide interim substitutes and be open enough to declare, within reason, the significant facts of his illness. It is best to say something reassuring if possible; however, if dealing with a malignancy or another impending or inevitable fatality, this must be handled in a straightforward manner. It is reasonable to make clear provisions for the patient with another therapist and to leave adequate records, as well as providing for coverage on an emergency basis.

In the face of serious illness, the decision of how long one should remain active in treating patients is based on many variables, and may require consultation with a colleague in terms of exploring significant issues and perhaps reality testing.

When the analyst returns to his practice after a prolonged illness, it is best if, at first, he observes an anonymity about his illness, to elicit the patient's fantasies. This material, as any other, can be very useful in terms of achieving therapeutic ends. Eventually, it will be appropriate to inform the patient of the realities of the illness since mutual trust is essential to the therapeutic alliance and *dignifying the patient's realistic concerns is important.*

The patient is likely to be preoccupied with the analyst's illness for quite some time. This preoccupation usually does not make it any easier for the analyst himself to deal with his own affliction. Conversely, however, having helped any number of patients with physical illness, impending death, and other tragedies, the analyst or therapist has a chance to analyze his own problems in these areas far in advance, which may be helpful when he has to face them himself.

The analyst's incapacitation is a difficult situation for everyone involved. Our profession does not have the machinery of an organization that will take the responsibility of intervening if the individual can no longer perform his job, be he too depressed, too psychotic, too physically ill, or too senile. There is no perfect answer, hardly any answer at all now, but peer review may eventually play a role. Recognizing and acknowledging limitations is a difficult issue, but it is the same in the superannuated, doddering Senator who continues to decide on vital issues of government, or more commonly, the individual who continues to drive a car when the senses and reflexes are greatly impaired. It is a tragedy to deprive someone of his livelihood, etc., but if his decisions and behavior can affect others in important ways, it poses a danger to individuals and the world when ability and judgment are compromised, for whatever reason.

Ernst Kris furnished an outstanding and dramatic example of the seriously ill analyst with responsibility toward his patients. After his second coronary he realized that he did not have long to live. He spent his last days in an oxygen tent dictating progress notes on his patients.*

DEATH OF THE THERAPIST

We have already discussed the circumstances involved in the serious illness, threatened fatality and impending death of a therapist. If a therapist actually dies, possibly suddenly, certain routines have been found useful. Usually, two or three friends and colleagues take it upon themselves, often at the surviving spouse's invitation, to divide the caseload among themselves and to call patients and inform them suitably about the therapist's death and offer their help in the transition. Usually it is best if each patient is seen by one of the friends or colleagues. If there were records, it is best to make use of them, to peruse them, before seeing the patient and then evaluate the patient's reactions and wishes and plans. Under some circumstances, it will be necessary to offer emergency psychotherapy to a patient who is acutely disturbed by the death. This may simply provide a transitional means of helping the patient until another permanent therapist can be found. All the dynamic factors we know about in grief and mourning are likely to be present and have to be worked through. In addition, it is rather frequent to find a great deal of rage over having been deserted by the deceased. The new therapist must be prepared for a full barrage of negative transference feelings which actually are meant to be directed at the deceitful dead therapist.

In the absence of a spouse and/or colleagues and friends, an organization to which the therapist belongs frequently plays the necessary role in making help available to the patients so bereaved.

As usual, a dramatic event is likely to have some positive fallout in terms of new insights derived from reactions to the therapist's death.

---

* Personal communication.

28. Problems of Psychotherapy as a Profession

The practicing analyst or therapist suffers many stresses to his own psychic apparatus and to his realistic adjustments which are unique to his profession.

The constant pull of regressive forces is always evident. In *Analysis: Terminable or Interminable*, Freud (1937) recommended that members of the profession should be reanalyzed every few years because the patients engender a regressive tendency. Generally, people are able and entitled to repress, including whatever emerges in analysis. In fact, if all goes well, the analysand should not become a walking textbook, constantly monitoring himself; he should have attained a certain automaticity by his restructuring, part of which is repression. In the psychotherapeutic profession, however, repression is constantly interfered with because the therapist must keep his primary process, his preconscious thinking, close enough to the surface to work with patients on this level of communication. Furthermore, in participating vicariously in the patient's problems, there are, directly and indirectly, many pulls and tugs on emotions, in terms of the patient's behaviors and transference. Patients can arouse anger, sexual feelings (particularly if they *want* to be seductive), much sadness, of course, and the full range of affects likely to appear in any such treatment. Hour after hour of such exposure has to have a marked effect on the therapist.

Unlike other people in different life situations, it is a crucial part of the analyst's job to maintain a passive, expectant position, coupled with the frustration tolerance and impulse control necessary to support such an attitude. Therapeutic neutrality, genuine frustration tolerance and impulse control are essential to perform the job and to withstand the various emotional conflicts, but susceptibility and responsiveness to these forces must be maintained and this takes its toll. Empathy plays an outstanding role in the entire therapeutic process, but tends to be exhaustive at times.

After spending eight hours in the office with patients (and most of us spend more), exhausting all affective and empathic resources, there is often little emotional availability left over when the analyst or therapist comes home to his family. The family members will have had their own stresses during their day, but most likely of a quite different kind, and therefore have different emotional needs. A child's world has its own problems, and the emotional burdens of a spouse in another field, for instance business, with its open competitiveness, are also great. Business activities, however, provide manifest active interchange; in psychotherapy the manifest relationship is more of a one-way street, leading to a peculiar kind of depletion. As a result, the analyst or therapist often cannot meet the emotional needs of his family.

The psychotherapeutic profession also presents many social manifestations of its particular occupational hazards. A great number of psychotherapists seem to wish to avoid intellectual films, dramatic theatre, or black comedy, though there are always some for whom artistic interest overrules everything else. Most, however, prefer lighter entertainment, feeling that they have had enough of the human tragicomedy all day long and don't need it in cinematic or theatrical forms. This sentiment is especially troublesome if the analyst's spouse is not in the field and enjoys these types of entertainment.

Psychotherapists may also have difficulties in making and maintaining friends and acquaintances. While one must draw a line between the professional relationship and the social relationship, it is hard to say to a friend under stress, i.e., in mourning or deeply frightened about a serious illness, "Look, talk to another psychiatrist or psychotherapist; don't talk to me." Because of his particular profession, the psychotherapist as friend can too easily become the psychotherapist as professional. Even though he may relate differently to a friend or relative in trouble, as compared to the way he relates to a patient, the similarity of his roles is too great if the friend or child or spouse has emotional difficulties. The experienced therapist learns, more or less well, not to respond analytically in a social setting, but this task is particularly difficult for the younger members of the profession. Often, young or old, the only way one knows to deal with this burden is to distance oneself again. Such a process interferes with close involvements or good friendships.

In turn, if the psychotherapist, like everyone else, has fears, conflicts, or anxieties, he is not apt to talk to colleagues about them in a social atmosphere. He knows how similar *his* problems are to what his friend/colleague hears everyday in the office. Very frequently, he may also be reluctant to reveal his problems, since such revelation may impair his professional image. If he complains to friends outside the field, their main response is likely to be one of surprise that *he* has problems—an attitude which does not lead to confiding easily.

Unlike many other professionals—lawyers, other kinds of physicians, businessmen—the psychotherapist does not have the advantage of a "real" relationship with the people he treats. Also manifestations of gratitude from the people for and with whom he works have a very limited scope. He cannot accept presents, nor does he visit patients socially. Unlike other professionals, the psychotherapist is unable to have a continued friendly relationship with the people whom he has helped. An attorney who does well for his client in a business deal may get a percentage or shares in a business. He may enjoy lunch or cocktails with his clients and they may become good friends. These social benefits are unavailable to the therapist, who has to be concerned with resolving the transference. When the job is done, it is time to say good-bye, leaving only whatever professional relationship is appropriate, should the patient need to return to therapy.

The social isolation and emotional depletion and deprivation of the analyst-therapist need effective measures as a remedy. After a tiring day it is only too easy to withdraw into a book or some more work of one kind or another—handyman jobs, files, writing, etc.

Surely these activities have a restorative effect. Nevertheless, it is important to forego them at regular intervals in favor of some social-emotional contacts. Old friendships from pre-professional days—if one has any—are usually the most gratifying, the most direct. Friends outside the field with interests shared in some field or activity are a welcome change. Dance, music, theater are, of course, valuable experiences.

Carrying the burdens of our profession—*solo*—often makes them especially troublesome. When we started a small psychoanalytic society, I proposed that it be used for "bull sessions" of practical, clinical, theoretical, personal matters rather than listening to more papers. Unfortunately, the society grew so quickly that it promptly became another public forum.

It may be possible and necessary to form small discussion groups of five or six for the purpose of sharing socially and emotionally. This kind of group would be a reasonable substitute for the English pub, the Lawyers' Club, the Viennese coffee house, and above all, for the spontaneous friendly meeting possible before excess mobility and daily overload interfered with them.

In the future, I expect psychotherapy to be practiced in group form—small corporations consisting of psychologists, social workers, child psychiatrists and psychoanalysts and general psychiatrists. Such groups would automatically serve as a professional meeting ground and some human contact. Personal friendship would still have to be sought, in addition.

Finally, a look at the conventional mode of compensation—money. The psychotherapeutic profession is absolutely not the way to get wealthy. By definition, the dyadic relationship is a "one-horse" business. Marx has pointed out that in the capitalist system, the individual or corporation becomes rich by virtue of "surplus value." For example, an employer who has five people working for him pays each half as much as the profit they earn for him. An employer of

100 people keeps the extra profit of each of those 100 individuals. Paying workers less than they earn, keeping their surplus value, makes the owner wealthy.

Marx's idea is, of course, much too simple—and sometimes businessmen lose their investment. But, as an illustration of the shortcomings of psychotherapy as a business, the comparison is useful. In terms of this oversimplified scheme, the fact that psychotherapy involves a one-to-one relationship means that the concept of surplus value and profit does not apply. In addition, the moment the analyst ceases to sit in his chair, he stops having an income. Thus, illness, vacation, and even going to the barber or hairdresser, as the case may be, become expensive propositions.

Thus, while the cost to each individual patient is high (since only relatively few constitute the therapist's total income), and the fee for "just talking" or "just listening" is very visible, the therapist's income, as compared to other medical specialties, is small and limited in horizon.

In addition, there is relatively little increment from the apprentice years to senior status in the profession: there is just so much money that any given individual is able or willing to pay for "one hour."

THE CHOICE OF PSYCHOTHERAPY AS A PROFESSION

Many factors contribute to the choice of psychotherapy as a profession. Structured interviews for psychiatric residents or candidates reveal certain predominant patterns. Generally, a rescue fantasy plays a substantial role, and is especially apparent in males, beginning classically as a derivative of the oedipal constellation and the wish to rescue the mother. Another pattern that I have seen frequently in interviewing psychiatric residency applicants is that they have had a depressed mother. This fact may have fed their rescue fantasy, but usually these people also grew up with significant emotional deprivation because the mother was unavailable due to her depression. Possibly related to this situation, it seems that psychotherapy as a profession attracts an introspective person who had difficulties in adolescence, especially of a depressive nature. It seems that the need for succor turns into a need for nurture.

Another frequently seen personality pattern in those likely to go into this field is the individual with some difficulties in object relations. He or she is likely to be quite shy and introverted. Psychotherapy is structured so that there are certain rules to follow, making relating in this structured setting much easier than in the real world. The object relations are regulated and therefore not truly reciprocal. The therapist listens and analyzes the transference and countertransference, and that largely limits the social interaction. While a certain amount of passivity is a useful part of the analyst's character structure, it is too often excessive in some who enter the profession. They are sometimes so passive that they have difficulty exercising an essential role of their profession: having a clear-cut conceptualization (which means *active* thinking) and clear-cut strategy and tactics (which means *active* intervention). Unfortunately, some analysts take the attitude that all they are supposed to do is lean back and grunt every once in a while. This is a serious misconception of what the analyst's role should be, intensified by the passive character traits.

MANAGING THE PROBLEMS OF A CAREER IN PSYCHOTHERAPY

The ability to bear working day in and day out with very disturbed and sometimes unpleasant people in very difficult life situations necessitates a basic compassion for the human condition. My own compassionate outlook rests on a rather pessimistic base. I see all members of humanity as victims of their past and their biological limitations, essentially helpless vis-à-vis most forces, including illness and death. Freud's *Civilization and its Discontent* (1930) clearly states that the human being experiences some basic unhappiness because of the built-in conflict between reality, drives and superego. Everyone has had a childhood that has made him feel helpless, just by virtue of being small and by experiencing difficulty in understanding and mastering the environment. Various life crises and eventually old age inevitably make one again aware of this helplessness. In this sense, one can and must feel compassion for anyone, on the basis of a truly shared experience of vulnerability and pain intrinsic to the human condition.

This compassionate attitude can also help a therapist suspend ordinary value judgments, especially if he is trying to help a person who, by all social standards, is indeed undesirable. Concretely, it may be helpful to the therapist and useful to the patient to use the following formulation: "I (the therapist) don't have to like everything about you (the patient). There are parts of you that I am not fond of, but there are also other parts of you that I *do* like. One part of you is quite rational, but there is another part of you that irrational and disturbed. The rational part in you and I should be able to work together to do something about the part that causes you and others trouble. This part of your personality is responsible for causing you pain and difficulty, as well as for urging you to sometimes engage in asocial, antisocial, irresponsible acts. We have to try to work together on that particular irrational part of you and the specific factors that make you behave in destructive ways."

Not all psychotherapeutic work is painful or difficult. There is very genuine pleasure to be derived from helping people, especially from working with very disturbed people and situations. Even with the chronically ill, the limited goals of maintaining optimum functioning, minimizing exacerbations of illness in terms of frequency and/or duration, and facilitating some better adaptation are significant and can be personally gratifying.

In all instances, the intellectual pleasure of trying to understand how things hang together, how current symptoms and events in adulthood manifest common denominators with childhood, establishing what were Freud's major contributions—the continuities between waking and dreaming life, between normal mentation and neurotic or psychotic mentation, and between the conscious present and the less than conscious past—provides the analyst with a tremendously satisfying feeling of closure. Closure provides a sense of competence and mastery and the pleasure of good functioning. Some creativity is also involved, leading to satisfactions similar to those derived from artistic work.

In fact, there is no other profession that provides as much daily participation in the human drama, painful as it may be at times. The lives of our patients are indeed a kind of Greek drama, in which events and actions develop almost inevitably as a result of earlier histories; psychoanalytic insight and technique provide the only real chance for modifying the causal chain of events. In psychotherapy, affective understanding of what makes one behave the way one does leads to actual structural changes in the personality. This fact makes psychoanalysis a truly creative profession.

There are other advantages to be derived from the psychotherapeutic profession. Therapeutic activity invites mutual enlightenment and "mirroring." Listening to patients, one can recognize certain problems and patterns of one's own, by way of the therapeutic relationship and the countertransference. Again and again, the psychotherapist has a chance to analyze his own problems and gain new insights, seeing aspects of himself in his patients. This aspect of the profession helps one to grow continuously, to develop more compassion and to be more rational. In a very general sense, the practice of psychoanalysis and psychotherapy leads to a further expansion of consciousness. Some people try to achieve such expansion with drugs. For others, reading great literary works and identifying with the characters have a consciousness-expanding effect. However, none of these activities is likely to lead to as much increased awareness as is derived from the practice of psychotherapy.

Aside from the inherent reconstructive forces just described, there are other possibilities of dealing with some of the inevitable burdens of psychotherapeutic work. One is to vary the nature of the patients one treats and also to vary the specific type of therapy employed, as much as possible. If feasible, one should mix some analytic or long-term therapeutic patients with some in brief therapy, and also include in one's practice individual, conjoint and group therapy. It makes the work day easier if one sees patients of different age groups and, of course, of both sexes.

Since psychotherapy is such a solitary occupation, it is important to have research, teaching or administrative activities as part of one's weekly workload. Aside from providing for different kinds of emotional relationships, my prescription is based on Selye's (1956) basic recommendation that to mix different kinds of stresses is to decrease the sum total of stress one is exposed to.

Speaking of stresses brings me to a few words on the physical aspects of practicing psychotherapy—and what to do about them. Physical inactivity—sitting endlessly—in addition to the need for excessive affective and motor control, is a serious problem in the career of psychotherapy. It is very likely that incidents of low back pain, overweight, hypertension and coronaries are more frequent in psychotherapists than in many other professionals. While none of us knows the precise etiological relationship, it is reasonable to assume that ordinary precautions and avoidance of excesses of these problems are important. I firmly believe that at the very least, every psychotherapist should have several hours of vigorous exercise a week.

Following some of the basic suggestions outlined here may help to make you a more content, healthier psychotherapist, following the old dictum that there should be a sound mind in a sound body.

REFERENCES

FREUD, S. Analysis: Terminable or Interminable (1937). In *Collected Papers*, Volume 5, pp. 316-357. London: Hogarth Press, 1950.

FREUD, S. Civilization and Its Discontent (1930). *The Standard Edition of the Complete Psychological Works of Sigmund Freud*, Vol. 21, 64-125. London: Hogarth Press, 1954.

SELYE, H. *The Stress of Life.* New York: McGraw-Hill, 1956.

Index